Recent Research in Psychology

Steve Baldwin

Alcohol Education and Young Offenders

Medium and Short Term Effectiveness of Education Programs

Springer-Verlag
New York Berlin Heidelberg London
Paris Tokyo Hong Kong Barcelona

Dr. Steve Baldwin, Dip Tech; BA Hons; Dip Clin Psychol; MSc; PhD
Consultant Psychologist, Neighbourhood Networks Project, TACADE,
Salford M5 4QA, UK
and
Visiting Research Fellow, Polytechnic Southwest, Plymouth PL4 8AA,
Devon, UK

Library of Congress Cataloging-in-Publication Data
Steve Baldwin, 1957-
    Alcohol education and young offenders / Steve Baldwin.
      p. cm. — (Recent research in psychology)
    Includes bibliographical references (p.).
    ISBN 0-387-97507-1 (New York). —ISBN 3-540-97507-1 (Berlin)
     1. Alcohol and crime—Scotland   2. Differential equations. Partial.
  1. West, Beverly Henderson. II. Title. III. Series.
  QA371.H77 1990
  515'.35—dc20   90-9649

Printed on acid-free paper.

©1991 by Springer-Verlag New York Inc.
All rights reserved. This work may not be translated or copied in whole or in part without the written permission of the publisher (Springer-Verlag, 175 Fifth Avenue, New York, NY 10010, USA), except for brief excerpts in connection with reviews or scholarly analysis. Use in connection with any form of information storage and retrieval, electronic adaptation, computer software, or by similar or dissimilar methodology now known or hereafter developed is forbidden.
The use of general descriptive names, trade names, trademarks, etc., in this publication, even if the former are not especially identified, is not to be taken as a sign that such names, as understood by the Trade Marks and Merchandise Act, may accordingly be used freely by anyone.

Text prepared on Xerox Ventura Publisher using author-supplied WordPerfect disks.
Printed and bound by Edwards Brothers, Inc., Ann Arbor, MI
Printed in the United States of America.

9 8 7 6 5 4 3 2 1

ISBN 0-387-97507-1 Springer-Verlag New York Berlin Heidelberg
ISBN 3-540-97507-1 Springer-Verlag Berlin Heidelberg New York

Preface

Since the establishment of the first alcohol education course (AEC) for young offenders in 1981, this form of service delivery has been expanded across the United Kingdom. While some before-and-after data have been reported, no controlled evaluations have been completed on effectiveness with this type of intervention.

The present research reports a series of evaluation studies to investigate the impact of AECs on offending and drinking behavior. Young offenders were recruited from local courts.

The first study, completed in Dundee, reported results from a comparative evaluation between two types of AECs. As an attention-placebo study, one group received a behavioral AEC with program contents designed to reduce drinking and offending behaviors. Some dependent variable differences between the two groups were observed at follow-up.

The second study was established in Glasgow as a replication of the main study.

The third study used a quasi-experimental design to establish a no-intervention control group in the Perth courts. Young offenders were recruited to complete screening interviews, without any intervention. The intervention group was recruited from courts in Forfar, a similar rural town. This group completed an information-based AEC, using educational materials about alcohol and its effects. Some dependent variable differences were observed at follow-up.

The fourth study was based in a Young Offender Institution at Forfar. Prerelease young offenders were randomly assigned to either a no-intervention control group or a behavioral AEC group. Some dependent variable differences were reported at follow-up.

Data from single-case studies and long-term follow-up data from the original Dundee study in 1982 are also reported.

Acknowledgments

This work was completed with financial support from the Alcohol Education and Research Council, Mathew Trust, Charity Projects, and Economic and Social Research Council.

Thanks to Diana Booth for layout, preparation and inspiration; to Wendy Janvrin-Tipping for proofreading, and to Ann Crawshaw for revision, formating, and dedication.

Acknowledgments to Nick Heather, David May, George Fenton, Ray Hodgson, Alan Lawson, Carol Greer, Jimmy Mooney, Sandy Gamba, Andrew Kerr, Frankie Braggins, John Cuthbert, Douglas Allsop, Linda Cousland, Sheriff John Wheatley, Sheriff Stuart Kermack, Sheriff John McInnes, and Sheriff Graeme Cox, Phil Barker, Mary Ward, Fraser Watts, Chris Colburn, John Christiansen, Judy Graham, the late Ron Creamer, Tayside Social Work Department, Tayside Police Department, the Noranside Governor, and the young offenders who participated in the evaluation study.

Thanks to Batsford Academic for permission to reprint material from "Alcohol Education and Offenders."

Contents

Preface		v
Acknowledgments		vii
1	The Context	1
2	Alcohol and Offending Behavior	15
3	Alcohol Education and Interventions	27
4	Alcohol Education Courses	36
5	Dundee	50
6	Glasgow	69
7	Perth/Forfar	76
8	Noranside	87
9	Kilmarnock	98
10	Discussion	104
11	Conclusions	125
Bibliography		137

1

The Context

History and Development

Contemporary responses to young adult offenders with drinking problems do not reflect the major shifts that have occurred in the alcohol field since the 1950s. Indeed, the range of legal and social responses currently available to such persons in the United Kingdom seems to reflect historical and dated views, both of offending behavior and of alcohol problems. Thus, despite shifts in the conceptualization of the development of alcohol problems and subsequent intervention programs (Heather & Robertson, 1986), responses to young adult offenders frequently have been limited to stereotyped, dated ideas (McGuire & Priestley, 1985). Although not restricted to the forensic services, this gap between theory, research, and practice has fostered an atmosphere of stagnancy and stunted growth.

Twenty years have passed since a pioneering epidemiological survey of drunkenness offenders in London Magistrates' Courts (Gath, Hensman, Hawker, Kelly, & Edwards, 1968). It has been sobering to note the failure by statutory agencies to respond to this landmark survey. This report noted the inadequacy of the existing provision for offenders, and indicated the urgent need for a "rehabilitation" service based on hostel accommodation. First offenders were identified as a group that required particular attention for early intervention.

Given the climate at the time when this report was published, it is at first surprising that progress in the forensic services has been so markedly retarded. The Criminal Justice Act, which became law the previous year (HMSO, 1967), had given urgency to such interventions in the penal system for persons who habitually committed offenses involving drunkenness. Moreover, the Act was innovatory in proposing the abolishment of the "drunk and disorderly" offense, contingent on the provision of alternative accommodation for offenders. Furthermore, there was a background climate in Western Europe and the United States to decriminalize drunkenness by excluding the offender from the courts and responding to the problem with medical/psychiatric services (e.g., Camberwell Council on Alcoholism, 1968).

This trend toward medicalization of offenders with drinking problems was evident in the recommendations of other reports (e.g., Pittman, 1968). Most researchers attempted to "classify" offenders with alcohol problems into one of the five categories of "alcoholism" (sic) produced by Jellinek (1960). Thus, in one epidemiological study it was observed that "50% of the offenders were suffering from the disease of alcohol addiction" (Gath et al., 1968).

Despite this medicalization of offenders, however, it was not always assumed that conventional hospital treatment would meet the needs of the person. Some medical practitioners were attempting to provide supportive environments in nonhospital settings (e.g., Cook, Morgan, & Pollak, 1968).

Whereas these hostel and detoxification centers were designed as an alternative to institutionalization, however, there was a clear emphasis on a disease model and an associated belief that such offenders "should be cast in the sick role" (Gath et al., 1968). The consequences of allocation and adoption of disease analogues are well known (Scheff, 1965; Szasz, 1962). The medicalization and subsequent "territorialization" of provision for offenders by physicians may explain some of the stasis in forensic services in the past 20 years. Thus, while decriminalization of drunkenness offending was a progressive initiative, the subsequent shift to medical/psychiatric perspectives may have been retrogressive.

This trend toward increased medicalization of the personal and social problems of drunkenness offenders continued into the 1970s. The supportive climate of opinion was such that this service provision for offenders was reflected in social policy measures both in the United Kingdom (HMSO, 1972) and in the United States (Alcoholism, Treatment and Rehabilitation Act, 1971). The predominant view of specialist agencies stated that drunkenness should not be subject to the judiciary processes; rather, it was considered to be an "illness," subject to medical treatment. This climate of medical expansionism also was fueled by a growing disenchantment with repeated fining and imprisonment of drunken offenders (Chafetz, 1971; Driver, 1969). There was a growing belief that the police, courts, and correctional institutions were severely overburdened, and that reform was overdue.

In the context of this medicalization of forensic services, some attempts were made to measure the perceptions of offenders about their offending behaviors. One study attempted to establish whether offenders perceived themselves as "bad or ill or both or neither" (Hershon, Cook, & Foldes, 1974) so that consideration could be made of "mass education or even coercion in an attempt to make efficient use of the new medical institutions." This study revealed that self-acceptance of the offender viewing themselves as an "alcoholic" (sic) "increased the likelihood of the researcher recommending some further action." Only a few drunkenness offenders conceived of their problems as an illness, however; they rarely used medical or psychiatric services for their drinking problems. Thus, while drinking was viewed as a learned behavioral response to a variety of personal and social pressures, self-perception as an "alcoholic" was considered by physicians to be a prerequisite for a positive response to intervention.

Thus, the predominant belief was that offenders should view themselves as suffering from a "disease" (sic) and accept the consequences of their subsequent "illness" (sic) before service provision was made available. Drunkenness behavior need not always be viewed as the "symptom of the disease of alcoholism." To view alcohol problems as a disease was conceptually invalid; by considering drunkenness as a learned behavioral response, however, it was possible to decriminalize the offense without invocation of disease concepts. This radical view was supported by research data that suggested that the consumers of such forensic services (i.e., offenders) did not perceive themselves (or their problems) in medical terms (Hershon, et al., 1974).

This move toward decriminalization of drunkenness offending, compounded by serious doubts about the utility and validity of medical/psychiatric perspectives, required a reappraisal of the contributions offered by other professional groups. In particular, workers with social sciences training and qualifications (e.g., clinical psychology, social work) had begun to challenge established practice (Prins, 1973; Schwartz & Goldiamond, 1975). This shift by statutory agencies away from responses restricted to *punishment* (criminal) or *treatment* (medical/psychiatric) interventions was associated with the development of alternative responses based on *practical help* for offenders (Trasler, 1974).

Public Order/Social Policy Responses to Criminal Behavior

There is extensive evidence that much of human behavior is rule-governed (Harre & Secord, 1972) and that social rules function in the interest both of individuals and groups. These rules also exert control over individuals and groups. These rules exert control over individuals with both prescriptive and proscriptive influences that alter the probabilities of specific behaviors. Paradoxically, offending behavior produces not merely negative consequences (e.g., loss or damage for the victim) but also positive consequences (e.g., reminders to nonoffenders about social boundaries). The search to produce a consistent response to offending behavior that is effective, humane, and rational has been elusive in Western society. In particular, it has been difficult to establish a penal code to provide an appropriate balance between (a) the needs of the victim and (b) modification of the behavior of offenders (Priestley, 1977). This may relate to a trend toward examination of multifactorial approaches to understanding the person rather than a consideration of actual offending behaviors.

An historical examination of social policy responses to offending behavior reveals that the predominant force was punishment in 18th and 19th century Britain. The aim of these interventions was to reform the individual offender by control of actions rather than social changes or methods of restitution (Foucault, 1979; Ignatieff, 1978). Contemporary responses to criminal behaviors reflect an inclusion of both treatment *and* practical help, although the ethos of punishment of individuals remains dominant. The range of such responses in Britain has included custody (community homes, detention centers, youth custody centers, prisons); probation (licenses, supervision orders), alternatives to prison (day centers, hostels), intermediate treatment (IT), community service orders (CSO), fines, cautioning, suspended sentences, and binding over the person to keep the peace.

Although most penal responses have been based on punishment, the influence of medicine and psychiatry has increased options based on "treatment" of the individual. The aim of such "treatment" interventions has been based on individual "rehabilitation," including chemotherapy, group therapy, individual psychotherapy, individual casework, and therapeutic communities. Such initiatives presuppose a "defect" that may be ameliorated by psychiatrists, psychologists, social workers, probation officers, or counselors (Price, 1978). These "treatment" perspectives are similar to "punishment" initiatives; both locate the source of the problem and the locus for change *within the individual* (Schur, 1973).

The provision of practical help for offenders has not been based on beliefs about the need for punishment or on assumptions about defects. Instead it has been designed to add skills or experiences for people who frequently have been deprived of opportunities to acquire such knowledge, by virtue of restricted education or limited learning environments. This approach does not depend on a particular theoretical perspective, instead adopting the view that offenders ideally should receive these opportunities as of right, in a society that previously has denied them these options (McGuire & Priestley, 1985). Such initiatives have included skills training and rights advocacy, prerelease preparation for inmates, "training for freedom," and remedial education. This provision has been based on beliefs about individual deficits that seek to increase the ability of offenders by adding to their repertoire of skills. Although not dependent on a formal scientific theory, this approach has been consistent with a social learning perspective (e.g., Mahoney, 1974).

With regard to penal effectiveness, there has been scant evidence that "punishment" is an effective mechanism of behavior change. In the United Kingdom, Home Office statistics have revealed that 87% of offenders aged 17 to 20 years (and 72% of offenders aged 21 to 29 years) sentenced to less than two years will have been reconvicted within five years (HMSO, 1969). For most young adult offenders, recidivism rates have been approximately equal, irrespective of type of court intervention. Indeed, some evidence has suggested that the apprehension of juveniles itself produces *more* delinquency behaviors (Gold & Williams, 1969). Moreover, crime rates have continued to increase steadily, despite any supposed "deterrent" effect of harsher sentencing policies (Radzinowicz & King, 1979). This has led to some demands for prisons to abandon their "rehabilitative" mission (Tittle, 1974).

Evaluation of "treatment" attempts to modify offending behavior has been made difficult by methodological inadequacies of previous research. The bulk of evidence, however, has suggested that recidivism rates have been almost unaffected by treatment interventions (Bailey, 1966; Brody, 1976; Davidson & Seidman, 1974). A review of this field (Blackburn, 1980) has suggested that the best results have been obtained when interventions have been directed at specific groups of offenders (e.g., Jesness, 1975; Shaw, 1982; Sinclair, Shaw & Troop, 1974). Attempts to modify actual offense behaviors also have produced some promising results (Sarason, 1978).

Few attempts have been made to evaluate the effectiveness of initiatives offering practical help to offenders. The available evidence has been inconclusive. Some research has suggested that recidivism rates are *unchanged* by this type of intervention (Priestley, McGuire, Flegg, Hensley, Welham, & Barnitt, 1984); other studies have suggested that acquisition of educational and job-related skills may help to lower reoffending rates (e.g., Lipton, Martinson, & Wilks, 1975). Attempts to evaluate the effectiveness of "practical help" approaches have been limited by the same restrictions imposed by methodological weaknesses common to reports of "punishment" or "treatment" initiatives. With few exceptions, most programs have failed even minimal research criteria of: clear program definition, replicable methods, control group, or two-year follow-up (Blackburn, 1980).

Neither "punishment" nor "treatment" approaches have provided cost-effective or efficient methods for intervention. This has increased the need for appropriate methods to reduce recidivism rates that directly examine the offense behaviors. This requires work with individual offenders (or small groups) who wish to change their behavior patterns. This approach involves consideration of the attitudes, beliefs, values, and behavior of the individual offender (Blackburn, 1985). Furthermore, an appreciation of the environment in which offending behavior has occurred requires eventual modification of penal codes and practices to complement and support changes that have occurred in individuals (Taylor, Walton, & Young, 1973).

Role of Alcohol in Offending and Secondary Prevention

The salience of alcohol in offending behavior is well established, and public intoxication has remained a criminal offense for more than 350 years. Whereas the rate of arrests was far higher in the 19th century than at present (Edwards, 1970), there has been a steady increase in "alcohol-related" crime in more recent years. Recorded offenses for public drunkenness in England and Wales have risen from 75,000 in 1968 to 82,961 in 1971; 109,691 in 1976; 98,301 in 1983; 67,567 in 1986; (HMSO, 1968). Moreover, alcohol has been linked with other criminal behavior such as murder (Gillies, 1965; Virkkunen, 1974), rape (Johnson, Gibson, & Linden, 1978; Rada, 1975), assaults (Roizen, & Schneberk, 1977; Thum, Wechsler, & Denone, 1973), spouse/child assaults (Gayford, 1978; Hanks, & Rosenbaum, 1977), and violent crime in general (Evans, 1980). Direct cause-and-effect links exist by definition with some offenses (drunk and disorderly, drunk and incapable, drunk-driving). Establishment of causal links between alcohol ingestion and other criminal behaviors has remained elusive (Jeffs & Saunders, 1983).

Detection of accurate base rates of drinking and/or offending behaviors also has been limited by methodological constraints. Some studies have focused on incarcerated offenders to obtain self-report data. This population, however, is not representative of all offenders who drink (O'Donnell, Voss, Clayton, Slatin, & Room, 1976).

All studies have indicated some relationship between alcohol and offending: 40% of English prisoners indicated "addiction" to alcohol (McGeorge, 1963); 65% of prisoners in Northern Ireland claimed a history of alcohol problems (Robinson, Patton, & Kerr, 1965); 50% of English prisoners indicated "serious" drink problems

(Gibbons & Silberman, 1970); 68% of English prisoners claimed to have been drinking prior to offending (Edwards, Grattoni, Hensman & Peto, 1976); 63% of prisoners in a Scottish Young Offenders Institution were intoxicated while offending (Heather, 1981). Despite limitations imposed by self-report accuracy, demand characteristics of interviews and problems with operational definitions (e.g., "addiction," "serious drink problems"), between one half and two thirds of incarcerated offenders perceived a relationship between alcohol ingestion and subsequent offending behaviors.

The drinking behavior of young adult offenders has been the focus of specific research activity. Researchers have examined the use of qualitative and small-scale studies (e.g., institutionalized populations) and also have focused on surveys based on large representative samples, with increasing use of longitudinal studies. Epidemiological methods have been applied to general populations in an attempt to eliminate selection biases of institutionalized or deviant populations. Research emphasis has examined patterns of "normal" use of alcohol as well as "abusive" patterns and development of alcohol-related problems. It has been difficult, however, to establish empirical criteria to define actual patterns of usage (Kandel, 1975), and several conflicting definitions have been proposed (e.g., Cahalan & Room, 1974; Celanto & McQueen, 1978; Miller, 1976).

The utility of a focus on young adult offenders who drink has been confirmed by evidence derived both from cross-sectional, epidemiological and longitudinal surveys (Kandel, 1980). Drug use (both licit and illicit) peaks at ages 18 to 21 years (Abelson, Fishburne, & Cisin, 1977; Johnston, O'Malley, & Eveland, 1978; O'Donnell et al., 1976; US Bureau of Census, 1978). Peak use of alcohol (and illicit drugs) occurs when juveniles enter young adulthood, before making commitments to family and work roles. Whereas cultural differences modify these generalizations, there is evidence to suggest that completion of education, entry into the labor force, marriage, and parenthood exert considerable influence over drinking patterns. Conversely, a variety of delinquent activities may commonly precede, but not cause, drug usage (Igra & Moos, 1977; Jessor, 1987; Jessor & Jessor, 1977; Kandel, Kessler, & Margulies, 1978).

Although absolute numbers of young adults who drink are high, relatively few young persons who drink are charged with offenses connected with violations (e.g., underaged drinking) of licensing laws (Vingilis, 1981). Several attempts have been made to determine whether these young persons who have been apprehended are also "problem drinkers" (e.g., Smart & Goodstadt, 1977). An absence of consistent operational definitions for "alcohol-related offending" or "trouble with the police due to drink" has made these investigations difficult and has prevented conclusive analysis.

"Alcohol-related offending" has been variously defined both as (a) crimes that presuppose use of alcohol (e.g., minor possession, drunk-driving, drunkenness), and (b) any offense that has been committed while intoxicated. In the first category, alcohol use or abuse determines subsequent offending behavior; in the second, the offending behavior is of most interest, with intoxication a secondary consideration. In addition, some alcohol-related crimes (e.g., drunk-driving, assault, criminal damage) are considered to be more "serious" than other minor offenses, because of consequences not only for the offender but also for other persons in the neighborhood (Sterne, Pittman, & Coe, 1967).

Unresolved methodological problems have confounded previous attempts to establish clear links between alcohol consumption and delinquency behaviors. Few studies have attempted to control for confounding variables that also influence drinking behavior of young offenders. In addition, there have been difficulties with terminology and definitions of "problem" or "heavy" drinking that have been used inconsistently. This has restricted legitimate comparisons between studies and limited generalizability of findings. "Social complications scales" have been used to determine problem drinking in delinquent and nondelinquent populations, although such attempts sometimes have confounded dependent and independent variables (Vingilis, 1981).

Other research studies have failed to specify variables such as age of the drinker; for example, endorsement of "twice a week" questions about drinking behavior has different consequences for a 10 year old child than for a person who is 18 years old. Most studies, however, have collapsed age into standard mean scores (e.g., MacKay, 1963; Pearce & Garrett, 1970). The validity of this approach has been questionable.

Almost without exception, most studies in alcohol use/abuse by young adults have limited validity, by virtue of absence of appropriate control groups. In addition, most research studies that have used such groups have controlled only for offending behavior; in reality other factors (e.g., age, sex, socioeconomic status, education, employment status, race, interview location, interview method, interview characteristics) all require more critical examination. Moreover, it has been extraordinarily difficult to control for "offending behavior" itself. Sample biases have existed in previous research on delinquency because drinking alcohol while attempting a criminal act may have increased the probability of detection and subsequent apprehension. More drinking offenders are detected than offenders who do not drink; this phenomenon will have biased research samples to suggest that apprehended offenders have been heavier consumers of alcohol. Resolution of this confounding variable, however, (while vital to research progress), has been notoriously difficult.

In summary, studies that have assessed drinking patterns of young adult offenders have not produced data that indicate a strong link between offending behavior and problem drinking. Development of sensitive instruments to permit uniform self-reporting and meaningful comparisons of offender and nonoffender populations has been slow. While in the data there have been some indications of high consumption levels of alcohol in young offender populations, this finding has been confounded with other variables (e.g., socioeconomic status). Most investigators have failed to specify adequately the types and seriousness of crimes committed, and whether or not crimes were alcohol related. Other research studies that investigated the drinking habits of young offenders (already charged with offenses related to alcohol) have produced conflicting results about levels of consumption relative to young offenders who do not drink and young persons who have not committed offenses.

There has been some suggestion that young offenders with "alcohol-related" offenses do drink heavily; the relationship between offending behavior while intoxicated and problem drinking has remained unconfirmed because of methodological flaws of inadequate controls and small sample sizes.

Secondary Prevention Attempts

There has been much evidence that secondary prevention (interventions with people who have already developed alcohol-related problems) is both an appropriate and effective goal for some client groups. In particular, it has been suggested (Heather & Robertson, 1983a; Robertson & Heather, 1982a) that such interventions may form the treatment of choice for populations such as industrial referrals, drunk drivers and young persons with alcohol-related offenses. Paradoxically, whereas a favorable outcome may be possible with these groups, such persons are unlikely to seek assistance voluntarily because they have not yet experienced sufficient negative consequences from their drinking.

There have been difficulties, however, in attempting such intervention programs with these client populations, possibly because neither the clients themselves nor other persons consider them a suitable target. "At-risk" groups may not perceive themselves as vulnerable and may not voluntarily seek assistance for unacknowledged "problems" (e.g., Leathar, 1978). Cultural variations also may help to explain how atypical patterns of drinking behavior (considered "problematic" by researchers and outgroup peers) may be overvalued by particular indigenous populations of drinkers.

Secondary intervention programs with problem drinkers in industrial contexts have achieved good success rates. It is unclear whether this has been due to the early intervention itself (i.e., before problems become "serious") or whether due to "motivational" factors (i.e., coercion to reduce drinking) relating to fear of job loss (e.g., Dunkin, 1981). Similarly, secondary interventions with drunk drivers have produced conflicting results (Preusser, Ulmer, & Adams, 1976; Scoles & Fine, 1977; Swenson & Clay, 1980) with equivocal conclusions about the effectiveness of this approach.

Despite the frequent assertion of links between criminal behavior in young persons and existing/future alcohol-related problems, there has been scant research in this area. Most studies have had limited utility because of methodological inadequacies, although one study has reported data from an alcohol education course targeted at an unselected group of offenders (Blane, 1976). Irrespective of any impact of alcohol education on the subsequent offending behavior of client populations, the presence of other social and personal drinking problems (e.g., social isolation, work problems, physical illness due to alcohol ingestion) may justify such secondary intervention attempts (Robertson & Heather, 1982a).

Intervention attempts based on alcohol (or other drug) education requires consideration of both positive and negative outcomes from such programs, both for clients and other persons. In particular, education and information about alcohol may (a) *increase* use/abuse of alcohol, and (b) *increase* incidence of alcohol-related problems (e.g., offending behaviors). While secondary prevention attempts have been less vulnerable to criticism than education initiatives based on primary prevention (e.g., in schools), there has been widespread resistance to such attempts. This has related to the pervasive belief that the response to alcohol or other drug problems is to "play it cool" and discourage discussion among users or potential users (e.g., Morgan & Hayward, 1976; Wiener, 1970). Hence, any attempt to promote alcohol education for young offenders requires concurrent evaluation of effects on both subsequent drinking behaviors *and* offending behaviors.

Three types (or levels) of prevention have been identified: primary, secondary, and tertiary. Contrasting theoretical frameworks have been proposed as a rationale for prevention initiatives, including control theory and socialization theory (Bruun et al., 1975). Control theory has predicted a direct relationship between consumption levels of alcohol and alcohol-related problems; prevention attempts have been directed toward reduction of alcohol intake. Socialization theory has predicted a relationship between the learning and development of individuals, families, and neighborhoods; prevention attempts have been directed to knowledge, attitudes, beliefs, and values with respect to alcohol consumption. Most contemporary prevention projects have suggested conceptual adherence to socialization theory (Staulcup, Kenward, & Frigo, 1979). Many such projects have promoted "responsible decision making" and skill acquisition to assist informed choices about alcohol ingestion (e.g., Education Commission, 1978).

A review of 21 primary, secondary, and tertiary prevention projects (Staulcup, et al., 1979) noted that most attempts relied on alcohol education to reduce misuse and related problems. All projects were based on the assumption that increased knowledge and improved attitudes about alcohol would prevent development of related problems. None of these projects, however, used random assignment of subjects (or control groups), and most were limited to measures of "alcohol knowledge" and "attitudes about alcohol." Moreover, none of the projects that offered alcohol education had demonstrated a link between knowledge (or attitude change) and subsequent drinking behaviors.

These research studies have been unable to resolve fundamental questions about the possible hypothetical deterrent effects of alcohol education on drinking. Some researchers have suggested that drug education may even stimulate alcohol/drug use or abuse (Jaffe, 1974; Stuart, 1974). Previous research in this field, therefore, has failed to resolve fundamental methodological problems, and has indicated the need for robust research designs, standardized measures and instruments, and a commitment to longitudinal programming and follow-up.

Similar investigators who have reviewed outcomes of alcohol and other drug education programs have concluded that the vast majority have been ineffective (Kinder, Pape, & Walfish, 1980). Some of the explanations for these apparent failures have been: (a) a lack of consensus on goals/objectives, (b) methodological/statistical inadequacies, (c) poor (or absent) evaluation of programs, (d) no identification of "active" program components, and (e) weak rationales that have assumed that increased knowledge will change attitudes/behavior (Freeman & Scott, 1966; Smart, 1976). Most research on alcohol education has suggested that presentation of "facts about alcohol" has not been a maximally effective strategy for attitude or behavior change (Stainback & Rogers, 1983).

This failure to achieve positive outcomes from a substantial research effort spanning more than 20 years has been due in part to an oversimplification of the process of behavior change. Successful alcohol abuse prevention requires more than mere provision of factual information; "alcohol education" is rather more similar to attempts at persuasive communication (e.g., Freeman & Scott, 1966). This process requires at least three phases: attention, comprehension, and yielding (attitude change). Thus, while education requires attention and comprehension, successful persuasion also requires the process of "yielding" (e.g., McGuire, 1969). This attitude change requires the presentation of information that is consistent with other beliefs and values.

The medium of alcohol education itself also has been investigated with reference to: (a) the recipient's view of the educational materials, and (b) the type of information about alcohol (e.g., positive and negative effects). Presentation of a two-sided message (i.e., where pros and cons are discussed) may be a more effective strategy in alcohol education programs (e.g., McGuire, 1969).

Other researchers have adopted a more generic approach to alcohol education and have established such efforts within the context of substance abuse prevention (Flay & Sobell, 1983). Thus, contemporary interest with skills teaching and skills-acquisition approaches has been viewed as a logical progression from previously oversimplified strategies that have failed to produce effective behavior change. Early attempts at alcohol education based on (a) moral objections, (b) fear approaches (Leventhal, 1970), (c) objective facts (Goodstadt, 1976), and (d) values clarification and decision making have not produced impressive results. Teaching an awareness of social influences that promote alcohol and other drug use (and acquisition of social skills to resist or cope with such influences) may be more successful (Duryea, 1983; Flay & Sobell, 1983). Consideration of sociocultural factors in prevention programs also has been acknowledged (Moser, 1979).

The establishment of "secondary prevention" programs with client populations such as juvenile and young adult offenders has increased research interest in this field. Indeed, the "early identification, referral or treatment of persons with alcohol problems" (Staulcup, et al., 1979) has been targeted as a necessary (and highly appropriate) focus for such attempts. Such alcohol education programs often have been offered to client populations as discrete "packages," although frequently it has been difficult to specify individual components of these packages.

Evaluation of such packages, compared with other approaches, has generated new interest in research on so-called "minimal interventions." Many research studies have concluded that problem drinkers often benefit from techniques such as bibliotherapy and/or self-monitoring, and do not always require intensive interventions (Heather & Robertson, 1983b; Miller, Taylor, & West, 1980). Some alcohol education interventions have achieved modest success with only minimal investments of resources (Duryea, 1983; Stainback & Rogers, 1983).

Controlled Drinking

Since the original report of resumed "normal" drinking in former chronic alcohol abusers (Davies, 1962), there has been substantial research evidence that cannot be adequately explained by traditional "disease" views of alcohol abuse (Heather & Robertson, 1983a; Pattinson, Sobell & Sobell, 1977). Irrespective of additional substantial empirical data that do not support disease conceptualizations, it also has become clear that it is neither useful nor parsimonious to view "deviant drinking" in this way (Robinson, 1972). In summary, the phenomenon is not "an irreversible disease, but rather a reversible behavioral disorder" (Heather & Robertson, 1983a).

Contemporary theoretical views of alcohol abuse (and of persons who abuse alcohol) have explained acquisition, maintenance, and resolution of problem drinking behaviors using social learning theory and behavior modification (Heather & Robertson, 1986; Hodgson & Rankin, 1976; Orford, 1986). One implication of adoption of a new paradigm for the alcohol field is that theoretically a goal of controlled drinking may be the "treatment of choice" for many drinkers with moderate problems; permanent abstinence from drinking has become the exception, rather than the rule. Although permanent abstinence might be regarded as essential for some persons with rare physiological abnormalities, many of the intellectual deficits observed in chronic alcohol abusers may be reversible, given a period of temporary abstinence. Moreover, some persons with a long history of alcohol abuse may require a protracted period of abstinence of 6 to 12 months.

The rejection of disease concepts, in favor of a behavioral understanding of alcohol problems, has helped to avoid the damaging secondary effects of labeling a person "sick" or "diseased." Behavioral explanations for problem drinking do not relieve the person of their responsibility for subsequent action; this has avoided some of the difficulties of the self-fulfilling prophecy of a disease model (Sobell, Sobell, & Christelman, 1972).

In addition, there has been scant support for the belief that the "general public" view of problem drinking and problem drinkers is based on disease/illness models (Dight, 1976; Haberman & Schienberg, 1969). Both public and professional attitudes have reflected the confusion that has continued in the alcohol field; while many people will endorse attitude statements about disease models, underlying beliefs and values indicate a more sophisticated understanding of addictive behaviors and their personal meaning to individuals.

Implications for intervention attempts and education initiatives have been considerable: a recent review of United Kingdom alcohol treatment units (ATU) and Councils on Alcohol (CA) found that 76% of the former and 50% of the latter offered controlled drinking intervention options (Robertson & Heather, 1982b). Although the survey was not exhaustive and subject to varying response rates, it indicated that controlled drinking had been adopted in part by many agencies in the United Kingdom. Other reports suggested that this has not occurred in the United States, where many practitioners and agencies have retained adherence to a "disease" model (Miller, 1983a).

Despite some claims that interventions with people who have alcohol problems are ineffective, such interventions can provide a context for change in other major life circumstances (e.g., health, employment, education, and housing). An option of a controlled drinking goal has helped people with drinking problems; such a range of choices has been shown to increase success rates (Parker, Winstead, Eilli, Fishger, 1979). In addition, increased awareness about controlled drinking may have encouraged more people to seek help for their problem drinking. Similarly, it has been possible to make more informed decisions when offering controlled drinking to clients for whom an abstinence goal is not appropriate (Heather & Robertson, 1983b). Also, agencies and practitioners have become more involved with clients who have early-stage problem drinking and those who have less severe associated problems.

A review (Heather & Robertson, 1983a) of controlled drinking treatments for problem drinkers suggested that levels of consumption can be reduced to acceptable levels of risk using brief interventions. Moreover, there has been some evidence that bibliotherapy and self-monitoring may be as effective as more intensive interventions with some problem drinkers (Heather, 1986b). An abstinence goal may be an appropriate intervention for early-stage drinkers, who do not have severe problems. It is only recently that this population has been considered as potential candidates for such interventions; this has increased research interest in "minimal interventions."

Most controlled drinking interventions have relied on the acquisition of skills or new learning to modify maladaptive drinking patterns. The emphasis on skill acquisition and knowledge via new learning has blurred some of the formal distinctions between "treatment" and "education." This may have helped to destigmatize interventions that help the drinker with moderate problems by provision of new information or skills. There have been some attempts to bridge the gap between "treatment" and "education" using brief advice, self-help manuals, and self-monitoring procedures (Miller & Munoz, 1976; Miller & Taylor, 1980). One implication of such "minimal interventions" in local neighborhood settings has been that many more professionals and nonstatutory workers have become involved in this provision.

Despite this trend toward more involvement with early-stage drinkers with less severe problems, however, often it has been difficult to recruit candidates for such intervention programs. Several studies have reported difficulties in recruitment of suitable clients for controlled drinking programs (e.g., Vogler, Compton, & Weissbach, 1976). Other researchers have accepted referrals from different sources (e.g., courts, industry) to overcome this problem. Many such programs have been completed in the United States with drunk drivers referred from the courts and there have been similar developments in the United Kingdom. Although there are ethical difficulties with compulsory interventions (Heather, 1976), an increase in the range of sentencing options to courts has potential advantages both for offenders and to wider society. The combination of techniques of social control and so-called therapeutic education, however, requires careful consideration.

Other interventions that have been used to bridge the gap between education and treatment have included employment-based programs in high risk industry (e.g., Tether & Robinson, 1986) and school-based programs for vulnerable groups (e.g., Weiss & Moore, 1986). These strategies have offered possibilities for "primary" or "secondary" prevention with at-risk groups, without redress to compulsory attendance. Both these options also have offered opportunities for evaluation of controlled drinking programs. Such services, however, are in their infancy, and the field has continued to develop without rigorous evaluations.

Minimal Interventions

One of the consequences of the shift in services away from specialist medical treatment centers has been a new interest in brief interventions by nonspecialist personnel in local settings. This trend has been consistent with conclusions from reviews of controlled drinking research, which has advocated such services for clients with less severe drink problems. In particular, use of self-help manuals, adoption of moderation goals, and use of behavioral self-management methods have added to the success of interventions with problem drinkers (Heather, Whitton, & Robertson, 1986). Indeed, failure to find differences between studies that have used minimal behavioral interventions and studies with more extensive comprehensive behavioral self-management strategies have suggested that intensive programming may not be appropriate for these client populations. In addition, therapist/counselor variables (e.g., empathy, personal warmth) exert a considerable influence on outcome (Miller, Taylor, & West, 1980) although this remains an underresearched area of enquiry.

Several interrelated themes have promoted the interest in minimal interventions: the demise of disease models, a shift toward services in local settings, deinstitutionalization movements, increased involvement among self-help and nongovernment organizations, findings of controlled drinking research, and cost-effectiveness considerations.

In particular, the shift from disease models toward social learning theory explanations for problem drinking (Hodgson, Rankin, & Stockwell, 1978), combined with the outcome data from controlled drinking studies, have reported effectiveness of self-help manuals and self-monitoring methods. Most of this research has been completed with clinic or hospital populations of "outpatients" (sic). It is only recently that clients have been recruited either from courts (e.g., Miller, 1978) or via media advertizing (Heather, Whitton, & Robertson, 1986).

Therapeutic possibilities for minimal interventions with young offenders with drinking problems encapsulate many of these themes. In particular, this client group offers opportunities for "secondary prevention" initiatives both in institutional and local neighborhood settings. Young men under 40 years of age (with few physical problems associated with drinking) may be candidates for a goal of controlled drinking, particularly those who are in regular employment (Heather & Robertson, 1983a). Some preliminary minimal intervention studies were completed with this client group (Robertson & Heather, 1982a) although controlled evaluation research has not been reported (Gamba, Baldwin, Greer, & McCluskey, 1989).

Moreover, a recent review of such services for young offenders in the United Kingdom revealed a wide gap between service provision and evaluation. A survey of 20 agencies found that while more than 1,750 offenders had completed an alcohol education course (AEC) since 1981, no evaluation research on effectiveness had been completed (Baldwin & Heather, 1987). Thus, despite the completion of at least 250 AECs, there have been no data generated on efficacy or cost-effectiveness. While some agencies have produced descriptive statistics in unpublished reports, the central questions of whether these AECs have exerted any effects on offending or drinking behaviors have remained unanswered.

Summary

Despite the firm establishment of AECs in 1981 as both an institutional and noninstitutional response to drunkenness offending, answers about efficacy questions remain unknown. In addition, the failure to resolve these central questions also has marginalized other important "secondary" variables such as setting, therapists, costs, and client characteristics.

Controlled evaluation of AECs has remained unaddressed in the United Kingdom since their inception as a service provision to drunkenness offenders in 1981. As a minimal intervention strategy with mass applications for thousands of young offenders in Great Britain, it has remained certainly not untried, but definitely untested.

2

Alcohol and Offending Behavior

After more than 60 years of scientific analysis, the nature of the link between alcohol and offending behaviors has remained imprecisely specified.

While most researchers and practitioners have been united in the belief that some link exists, the exact nature of this relationship has remained obscure. This failure to achieve rapprochement between theoreticians, researchers, and practitioners may be explained by several factors, including: methodological weaknesses, design flaws, an expansion of unevaluated fieldwork, and an absence of controlled interdisciplinary studies. To date there have been few signs of change toward a more integrated understanding of the link between alcohol and offending behavior.

Evidence for the link between alcohol and offending behaviors has been accumulated from several sources. For example, epidemiological studies of court statistics have indicated the presence of serious drinking problems among persons convicted for public drunkenness offenses (Gath et al., 1968). Prison surveys (while limited by the knowledge that incarcerated drunken offenders may not be representative of the whole population of drunken offenders) have indicated that more than 50% claimed a direct link between intoxication and incarceration (Heather, 1981, 1982). Offenders interviewed before a court appearance (after overnight detention) also perceived a strong link between their alcohol ingestion and subsequent offending behavior (Hershon et al., 1974). The knowledge that apprehension of offenders, in particular juveniles and young adults, may *increase* the probability of reoffending (Gold & Williams, 1969) has produced an additional dilemma for practitioners working at the alcohol/offending interface. Specifically, there has been a need for practitioners to demonstrate that the net effect of their interventions have not been negative. Similarly, studies that have examined the link between alcohol and offending behavior have failed to accumulate detailed knowledge of nonapprehended offenders. The evidence for the effectiveness of apprehension among juveniles and young adults has been equivocal at best (Gold, 1969; Gold & Williams, 1969).

The scientific study of the link between alcohol and offending behavior also has been impeded by widespread misconceptions and confusion about the proper domain for such study. The move to decriminalize drunkenness offenses during the 1960s and 1970s has been accompanied by a drift from a social-legal to a medicopsychiatric focus of enquiry (e.g., Hamilton, 1976; Mitchell, 1971). One consequence of this shift has been to alter the focus of investigations away from environmental determinants of behavior toward the individual offender and his/her drinking.

The search for this hypothetical link also has been retarded by a widespread belief in a single unifying model/theory, which would serve to rationalize interprofessional differences. Offenders, however, do not constitute a homogeneous population, and their drinking/offending behaviors do not always conform to predictable patterns (Blackburn, 1980). There is no single psychological, sociological, or biological model that will account for all drinking/offending behavior (Pernanen, 1982). To date, the study of the alcohol/offending interface has been impeded by a widespread failure to study a range of specific subpopulations of offenders: most studies have focused on incarcerated, detained, or highly selected groups of convicted offenders (Pernanen, 1982). An understanding of the alcohol/offending interface has been limited by an absence of knowledge about subpopulations of nonincarcerated, unconvicted offenders who drink (Stumphauzer, 1979).

Alcohol and Youthful Offending Behavior

The study of the relationship between alcohol ingestion and offending behavior has been retarded further by difficulties in collection of criminal statistics. In particular, the use of terms such as "alcohol-related offending" has been used to denote a wide range of criminal behaviors. A distinction is required, however, between offenses in which alcohol is *part of the crime definition* (drunk and disorderly) and those in which alcohol is an *accompaniment to the offense*.

The link between "offending behavior" and "problem drinking" also has remained obscure and the confounding of dependent and independent variables has blocked their analysis (Vingilis, 1981). The most serious methodological flaw, however, has been the virtual absence of appropriate control groups in most studies of the alcohol/offending link. Where comparisons have been achieved, such studies have focused on offending behavior; other salient factors such as age, sex, socioeconomic status, education, occupational status, and place of interview have remained virtually unexplored.

A recent review of the studies that examined the link among youthful offending behavior and "problem drinking" concluded that insufficient evidence existed to support such a link (Vingilis, 1981). Moreover, the methodological limitations of the term "alcohol-related" have masked the phenomenon of offending behavior: the use of offense titles such as "assault" would obscure the involvement of alcohol in the offense. Such idiosyncrasies of recording and detection of offending/drinking behavior have delayed scientific enquiry.

Other studies, which have explored social and personal characteristics, have suggested that delinquent youths involved in alcohol-related offending are similar to delinquents involved in nonalcohol-related offending, with the exception that the former group claim greater alcohol consumption (Nylander & Rydelius, 1973;

Wattenberg & Moir, 1956). Clear conclusions from research on this topic have been obscured by the confounding variables of police behavior and court sentencing procedures. There has been a virtual absence of empirical studies using adequate control groups and independent/objective measures of alcohol involvement, using instruments to assess comparisons of consumption between delinquent and nondelinquent youth.

Most studies that have investigated the nature of the link between alcohol and offending behavior have concluded that, whereas a correlation (i.e., a statistical association) exists, the relationship is unclear (Pernanen, 1982; Vingilis, 1981). Other investigators, however, have proposed a *causal* link between alcohol and offending, in particular with violent criminal behavior. Such analyses have suggested that alcohol consumption, although not the sole influence, should be viewed as one causal factor or a link in a causal chain (Lenke, 1982). This observation has been based on very strong statistical relationships found at the macro (i.e., societal) and micro (i.e., individual) level between alcohol ingestion and some violent offending behaviors. Although this analysis does not presuppose mechanistic connections between the two behaviors, it has elevated the role of "alcohol consumption" beyond simple statistical associations.

More recent demographic studies completed in a United Kingdom Magistrates' court with young offenders (Hawker & Stevenson, 1984) have replicated previous studies of a more general population of offenders (Gath et al., 1968). In particular, while self-reported measures suggested a clear statistical relationship between alcohol ingestion and subsequent public order offenses, individual offenders did not perceive an equivalent link. This failure to find a subjective link between alcohol/offending behaviors among apprehended (but nonincarcerated) offenders has replicated previous findings. Moreover, not only do young criminals *not* perceive a subjective link between alcohol ingestion and offending, but 70% of apprehended "public order" offenders did not see the need to "be more careful of their alcohol consumption in the future" (Hawker & Stevenson, 1984).

Such findings have challenged alcohol educators: while "scientific enquiry" has supported a strong statistical association, self-reports from demographic surveys and research investigations sometimes have denied this link. The apparent minimal impact of prior alcohol education (i.e., factual information provision) on the subsequent criminal behaviors of these public order offenders also has raised questions about the validity of similar approaches to behavior change.

Many studies that have investigated the link between alcohol and young offenders (i.e., juveniles and young adults) have been based on assumptions that suggest that the focus of the problem remains in the individual offender. In particular, this idiographic approach has focused on the individual as the source, origin, and cause of the problem as well as the appropriate site for remedial interventions (McGuire & Priestley, 1985). This failure to account for interactional variables, which include an appreciation of environmental influences, has dominated intervention attempts. One effect of this focus on individual offenders with drinking problems has been the promotion of intervention attempts designed to modify drinking patterns within this population. The promotion of AECs has been one development based specifically on a model of individual behavior change.

Although this focus on the individual risks noninclusion of environmental variables, it has produced a renewed interest in attempts to modify offending behavior directly. Although the ethos of intervention attempts with offenders has shifted from punishment to treatment to practical assistance (Foucault, 1979; Ignatieff, 1978), the focus has remained on the individual offender. The recent trend to provide practical assistance to a client group that typically has received a meager distribution of resources has nonetheless continued to focus on the individual person.

Conclusive evidence for these approaches has remained elusive; it is known, however, that punishment attempts (e.g., imprisonment) do not reduce recidivism rates. For most juveniles and young adult offenders, recidivism rates are approximately equal, irrespective of type of court disposal (McGuire & Priestley, 1985). Equally, imprisonment does not appear to reduce criminal behaviors. Reviews of various sentencing policies and rehabilitation programs suggest uniformly negative conclusions. This "failure scenario," however, has produced two suggestions for improvements: the need for a "differential intervention" paradigm, (matching clients to specific interventions) (e.g., Glaser, 1980; Glaser & Skinner, 1981) and a direct focus on offending behaviors (Blackburn, 1980).

This shift to a direct focus on offending behaviors has produced prerequisite conditions for such interventions. In particular, it has required self-selection of offender/clients who have wished to modify their own behavior. With regard to hypothetical stages of behavior change (Prochaska & Di Clemente, 1982) it has produced a focus on offender/clients who have reached an "action" stage.

The shift also has produced more specific attention to investigation and/or modification of the attitudes, beliefs, feelings, and behaviors of offender/clients. A recent review (Flay & Sobell, 1983) noted the systematic focus on attitudes, beliefs, decision making, and values clarification in various alcohol/other drug education programs in the United States. The most recent trend has been a return to the development of skills acquisition as the major single component of such programs. This is consistent with a similar trend to include more skills teaching in United Kingdom AECs (Baldwin, Greer, & Gamba, 1991).

Youth and Alcohol Use

Identification of the link between the alcohol ingestion/offending behavior interface requires consideration of drinking among nonclinical, noninstitutionalized populations of juveniles and young adults. Early classic reviews of studies of drinking behavior in adolescents produced findings of increased alcohol ingestion among males and an increased frequency of drinking with increased age (Stacey & Davies, 1970). Similar findings have been obtained in other studies, which have concluded that consumption of alcohol by juveniles is usually part of the normal process of socialization (Stacey & Davies, 1972). Other studies based on longitudinal data have extended these early findings. Demographic research from junior and senior high school students has suggested that "becoming a drinker" is an integral aspect in the development of adolescence. Moreover, many studies have not supported previous beliefs about deviant teenage drinking in a "gang culture"; adolescent drinking attitudes and behavior reflect adult norms (e.g., Jessor & Jessor, 1975) and peer behaviors (e.g., Kandel, Trieman, Faust, & Single, 1976).

A review of such studies concluded that attempts to modify the drinking behavior of juveniles and young adults would require modification of preferences, norms, and supporting beliefs via changes in expectations about alcohol (Biddle, Bank, & Martin, 1980). Other reviews of demographic and epidemiological surveys of alcohol/other drug use among youth have demonstrated definition problems. Terms such as "abuse" have several operational definitions and empirical criteria for various use/abuse patterns have not been stated; simple classification decisions have been made to categorize alcohol use and abuse from inadequate data. Nonetheless, research studies in the 1980s have produced a shift away from a focus on extremes to studies of use patterns in the normal population; small-sample institutional surveys have been replaced with large, representative, open-field surveys.

Prevalence studies have suggested that alcohol use is most intensive among the 18 to 24 year old age group; self-report data indicate that nearly 90% of young persons in their late teens acknowledge some alcohol use. The role of socioeconomic status and juvenile/young adult behaviors (e.g., drinking, criminality) has remained unspecified; most studies have failed to substantiate such a relationship (e.g., Jessor, 1980). The observed relationship between increasing age and declining use of alcohol/other drugs has been attributed to parental influences. Peak use of alcohol/other drugs occurs most often when youths enter young adulthood, at a time when commitments are developed to family (or work) roles. An inverse relationship has been hypothesized between age-appropriate social role participation and use/abuse of alcohol. Prevalence studies also have suggested that marital status may predict alcohol use rates: men living with women to whom they are not married have particularly high rates (Clayton & Ross, 1977). Furthermore, unemployed persons show highest usage rates of most drugs, in particular alcohol (e.g., Brunswick, 1979).

Several competing theoretical frameworks have been used to account for involvement of young people with alcohol. One attempt has used a socialpsychological approach to specify the joint role of environmental and individual forces in "problem-behavior proneness" (e.g., Jessor, 1987; Jessor & Jessor, 1977). Problem behaviors have been defined as those that deviate from age-graded norms. A second perspective based on social learning theory has attempted to merge psychological and sociological perspectives (Akers, Krohn, Lanza-Kaduce, & Rodosevich, 1979) to account for physiological and environmental influences. A third model has attempted to explain deviant behavior as a mechanism to promote personal self-esteem after devaluation experiences (Kaplan, 1977, 1978). The most parsimonious account, however, is contained in the framework of adolescent socialization theory (e.g., Kandel et al., 1978). This model has attempted to include both intragenerational (peer) and intergenerational (parental) influences, based on the social learning processes of imitation and social reinforcement.

A recent emergent theme during the 1980s has been the consideration of alcohol use and abuse within a developmental perspective. In particular, alcohol initiation and its early use has been viewed as a transitional behavior within the framework of normal development (e.g., Jessor & Jessor, 1977). Moreover, both quantitative and qualitative developmental processes feature in juvenile drinking patterns. In the former, the number of deviant acts may predict the occurrence of subsequent acts; in the latter, the nature of a prior act may predict a subsequent behavior.

Another major research theme during the 1980s has involved the increased use of longitudinal designs in the study of youthful alcohol use. Despite limitations imposed by funding restrictions, many researchers have adopted the longitudinal methodology using cross-sectional and cross-sequential designs to investigate drinking behavior in juveniles and young adults. These studies have been focused mainly on themes of etiology and prediction; most have been descriptive and most have been additive, not interactive. Despite these limitations, however, some predictor variables have been identified, based on intrapersonal attributes, and interpersonal influences. Intrapersonal variables that may predict future alcohol use include unconventional values or behaviors and rejection of social institutions which are often perceived as a lack of social controls.

Other predictors include nonconforming attitudes, declining school/work aspirations, and the occurrence of other behavioral precedents (e.g., property offenses). Interpersonal predictions include concurrent alcohol use among peers within particular "drug-specific" networks: prior association with users of a particular substance is the best predictor of individual use of that substance. Similarly, parental use of some alcohol beverages (e.g., spirits) predicts adolescent use.

An overview of recent trends in the field of longitudinal research on alcohol and youth suggests that the developmental perspective has been useful in studying socialization. Concepts of "stages" and "maturation" have assisted in the understanding of the role of different factors at different times during a behavioral sequence of substance use/abuse. Several research studies have highlighted the methodological circularity of reliance on "subjective" self-reports. Other observations have included a growing awareness of the failure to attend to concurrent changes in society, based on legal or social policy reforms.

Youth and Alcohol Abuse

Examinations of the drinking patterns of juveniles and young adults has been difficult, because of discrepancy and disagreement about terms such as "abuse" and "alcohol-related" (e.g., Vingilis, 1981). For example, whereas some adults regularly drink excessive amounts of alcohol, and do not consider it problematic, one single episode of drunkenness in a child will always be a problem (Addeo & Addeo, 1975). Moreover, while amount and frequency of alcohol ingestion constitute two salient behavioral variables, body size and tolerance also will alter the effects on the person. These definitions have not yet been satisfactorily resolved, and distinctions between "problem drinker," "excessive drinker," "social drinker," and "controlled drinker" have been the subject of much debate.

Consideration of alcohol abuse among juveniles and young adults has been further clouded by the compounding variable of adult denial (Hawkins, 1982). Specifically, adult researchers who have attempted to explain adolescent behavior may have developed "selective amnesia" and forgotten their own same-age behaviors. In addition, the increased social acceptance of alcohol has reduced the probability of it being viewed as an addictive drug; the toleration of alcohol abuse among adults has reduced the cultural acknowledgment of self-medication. Pervasive dual standards have endured attempts at social reform; in reality, a general desire to minimize aberrant drinking behavior has not been matched by a similar desire to eliminate such behaviors via technological/administrative modifications (Hawkins, 1982).

One effect of the provision by adults of vague, confusing messages about alcohol may be that juveniles attempt to attain adult status rapidly via emulation of drinking behaviors. The development of yet another dual adult value system (proscribed legal usage, within the context of ready access in the home) has increased the probability of age-inappropriate juvenile and young adult drinking patterns.

Insufficient recognition of these inconsistencies and irregularities in societal value systems has hindered progress in modifying juvenile/young adult problem drinking. Failure to exert an impact on reduction of problem drinking incidence among juveniles may have resulted from a failed recognition that drinking behavior will continue, irrespective of adult interventions. The failure to set achievable goals (e.g., controlled drinking, responsible alcohol use, "skilled drinking," moderate drinking, social drinking) instead of unachievable goals (abstinence for all) may have retarded progress (Hawkins, 1982). Effective prevention programs designed to counteract known forces in juvenile alcohol abuse (i.e., peer pressure in groups) have been developed too slowly. In addition, some alcohol educators and researchers have not developed the necessary skills to teach adaptive drinking patterns to juveniles and young adults (Keller, 1980).

Other epidemiological studies have investigated an hypothesized link between high consumption of alcohol, simultaneous use of other drugs, and offending behavior. Prospective follow-up studies, in particular, have identified high-risk juveniles with alcohol-abusing parents, school problems, and serious offending behaviors (Nylander & Rydelius, 1973; Rydelius, 1983a). These studies have generated an hypothesis that proposed "a group...which develops alcohol abuse in combination with drug abuse...shows early aggressive acting-out behavior, lack of control of impulses..." (Nylander & Rydelius, 1973).

The drinking behavior of young adults in the "normal" population has been examined in similar studies. In particular, many young men were interviewed about alcohol consumption, other drug use, offending behavior, and social/personal characteristics. Despite several methodological difficulties (e.g., false information, interviewer bias, recall for historical information), high-consuming juveniles seem qualitatively different from low-consuming juveniles (Rydelius, 1983b). Unfortunately, these studies have not indicated whether these variables preceded alcohol consumption or were the result of it; furthermore, it was not explained how alcohol abuse and offending behaviors had co-occurred.

Authors of prospective follow-up studies have concluded that young men who have been raised by (an) alcohol abusing parent(s) may react with impulsivity and acting-out of aggression: this group will be vulnerable both to alcohol/other drug abuse and offending behaviors (Rydelius, 1983a, b). The hypothetical link between these variables has been ascribed to the psychosocial behaviors of this population, who have tended to seek out the company of friends in the same situation. A circular pattern, involving deterioration of adjustment and increased probabilities of drinking and offending behaviors, has been proposed (Rydelius, 1983b).

Researchers of alcohol cessation studies among juveniles and young adults have suggested that abstinence is a high-frequency occurrence among users; specifically this behavior has been investigated to resolve the paradox of how some young persons develop abusive drinking patterns while others remain "problem-free" (Lanza-Kaduce, Akers, Krohn, & Rodosevich, 1984). Such studies have begun to explore how the social and pharmacologic properties of alcohol have both reinforcing and punishing effects. Equally, interaction groups and norms may provide mores for imitation of use or for abstinence. An understanding of the mechanisms of cessation may be required to modify abusive drinking styles: whereas some young persons can adopt reduced drinking patterns, some require abstinence (Heather & Robertson, 1983a).

Increased agency involvement with juveniles and young adults who have harmful involvement with alcohol has assisted the realization that early intervention is necessary and appropriate to arrest the development of further problems or disabilities. Although most such services have been developed from statutory agencies, some have started from the nonstatutory sector of self-help organizations (Pernanen, 1982). These services frequently have targeted clients with multiple drug abuse. Some negative predictor variables for program completion have been derived, including: disruption/termination/cessation of school (or employment), late entry to alcohol program, acting-out aggressive behaviors among males, and repeated arrests and convictions. Some have suggested that alcohol abuse may precipitate indiscriminate use of other drugs, mediated by impaired judgment and poor decision-making skills (Hoogerman, Huntley, Griffiths, Petermann, & Koch, 1984). A point of diminishing returns exists in intervention programs for juveniles/ young adult abusers.

More recent longitudinal research has suggested a secular trend toward increased alcohol abuse among juveniles and adults due to an earlier age of onset (Keyes & Block, 1984). Although conclusive evidence has not been available, similar trends toward earlier and more extensive abuse with other addictive substances among young persons has been noted. Moreover, the typical transition from legal to illegal substances (e.g., alcohol to marijuana) may have changed or may have been initiated earlier, due to the increased availability of narcotic drugs.

The Alcohol/Offending Interface

To date, many barriers have not yet been surmounted to specify the nature of the link between alcohol and offending behaviors. Specifically, there has been much reliance on the statistical associations between offending behavior and alcohol use/abuse (Pernanen, 1982). At best, however, this method of investigation can only provide information about correlations between behavior or events; statements about the possible *causal* influences are not possible. Moreover, many terms (e.g., "alcohol abuse," "crime") have remained imprecisely conceived and inconsistently applied, rendering operational definitions difficult.

Nonetheless, four distinct approaches have evolved: (a) traditional studies (e.g., accounts of per capita alcohol consumption, proportional to crime rates), (b) naturalistic experiments (e.g., studies of crime rate decreases, from decreased availability, following social legislation), (c) individual coincidence estimates (retrospective accounts of events that precede crime), and (d) experimental/clinical studies (fieldwork/exploratory investigations of actual analogue events). These differing approaches have produced a range of explanatory links between alcohol/offending behaviors based on direct cause-effect relationships, common-cause relationships and/or associative relationships. The wide range of explanatory frameworks has prompted the conclusion that no single, global theory can account for this complex relationship (Pernanen, 1982).

Although there has been some evidence for a causal role of alcohol in a chain of events preceding some specific violent behaviors (e.g., Lenke, 1982), it has been extremely difficult to extend such findings to demonstrate more general causative effects. Research data that are reliable, durable, and replicable have yet to be produced. One result has been a trend during the 1980s to investigate "common-cause" relationships (i.e., intervening variables). The hypothetical role of these intervening variables would be to increase the probabilities of *both* drinking and offending behaviors. Such "third variables" (e.g., "stress") have been used to account for dispositional factors that exert a mediating influence on drinking and/or offending. Some of the difficulties in specifying alcohol/offending links, therefore, have resulted from theoretical flaws.

Moreover, much theorizing has occurred in an empirical vacuum; the lack of careful specification of field-testing conditions may have produced exaggerated claims for the degree of association between alcohol and offending. Moreover, as different models may be valid under different empirical conditions, the need remains for rapprochement between the phenomenological and statistical viewpoints. In addition, this "theoretical tradition" may have promoted a narrow individualistic focus, to the exclusion of situational perspectives (Pernanen, 1982). The need to view theories and models as investigative tools, not an immutable scaffolding, remains paramount.

Summary

An overview of theoretical perspectives on alcohol/offending links suggests that imprecision, confusion, and disagreement have dominated the field. Failure to reconcile different viewpoints has been due to almost orthogonal theories and models as well as discrepant methods of inquiry. (For example, sociological "deviance" models, based on societal norms and behaviors, do not mesh readily with biochemical "excess/deficit" models, based on an idiographic study of individuals.)

The weakness of explanatory links may reflect the degree of discrepancy between theories of offending behavior and alcohol use/abuse. More recent attempts to provide broader explanatory accounts based on superordinate constructs may offer a rapprochement. Two examples include social learning perspectives (Marlatt & Parks, 1982) and transtheoretical models (Prochaska & Di Clemente, 1982, 1986).

Methodological Overview

Explanation of links between alcohol and offending have been used to determine: (a) the nature of the role of alcohol in offending, (b) the prevalence of alcohol problems among offenders and nonoffenders, and (c) the offending history of people who have drinking problems. The wide range of professional interests represented within these broad fields has ensured a multitheoretical consideration of research questions. As a negative corollary, however, the same wide range of interests may have retarded progress in the field.

In addition, several methodological research problems have remained unresolved. These have included: (a) loose (or multiple) definitions of "alcohol use/abuse," (b) multiple definitions of "criminal" activity, (c) sample bias in field experiments, (d) lack of adequate experimental controls, (e) insufficient data about context of drinking behaviors, and (f) a narrow focus on specific subgroups of offenders/drinkers (Greenberg, 1982).

Furthermore, several assumptions central to the alcohol/offending interface have not yet been empirically validated (e.g., that different types of alcohol exert similar psychoactive effects). Similarly, in the nomothetic search for an understanding of correlational/causal links based on group data, the salience of individual differences (e.g., in biological functioning) may have been overlooked (Pallone, 1988).

Some methodological problems have been population-specific. Many prison studies, in particular, have been subject to systematic distortions in data collection and subsequent interpretations, due partly to self-serving attributional biases among inmate offender/clients. Other forensic studies, such as data from police investigations, also have been flawed by reliability and validity problems. Inconsistent police reporting, an over reliance on offenders' verbal self-reports of drinking, and measurement problems of blood/alcohol concentrations have been confounding variables in several studies (Greenberg, 1982). Similarly, it has been extremely difficult to obtain valid and reliable information in courts about drinking behavior of offender/clients (Baldwin & Thomson, 1991).

Several other methodological problems remain unresolved. Specifically, (a) most studies have reported single-source data in their examination of drinking behavior, (b) distinctions between "presence of alcohol" and "intoxication" are unclear, (c) criteria for "drunkenness" have not been reported, (d) different data sources have been confounded, (e) inconsistent and vague definitions of "offending behavior" have persisted, and (f) prison studies have focused on "convicted offending-behaviors," to the exclusion of "unconvicted offending-behaviors." In addition, widespread confusion between the models used (vice, social problems, disease) has increased uncertainty about the competing conceptual definitions of people who have drinking problems (e.g., addict, "alcoholic," (sic), problem drinker) because of lack of agreed criteria (Sanchez-Craig, 1980).

Despite recognition of these methodological flaws, the assumption exists that a "single-variable direct-cause relationship underlies...research" (Greenberg, 1982). There has been a continued reluctance to abandon methods of very limited utility and applicability. Moreover, the continued striving and search for causality has been unrealistic, given the limitations of most studies, which have focused on single independent variables. Limitations of experimental designs instead have restricted their potency to statements about conditional probabilities. Inadequate selection and implementation of control/comparison groups have compounded these problems; this has perpetuated uncertainty in a research field where fundamental questions (e.g., the sequential ordering of drinking/offending behaviors) remained unanswered and largely unaddressed.

Consideration of methodological trends in alcohol/offending research has identified three main areas for evaluation: (a) the role(s) of alcohol in offending behavior, (b) the prevalence of alcohol problems in offenders, and (c) the offending history of people who have drinking problems. Investigation of studies in this area suggests the influence of six dominant biases in the research process: (a) hypothesis selection, (b) sampling, (c) selection of clients, (d) definitions (e.g., "drinking behavior)," (e) experimental design, and (f) data analysis. In addition, much of the existing research has been based on self-report measures, without physiological correlates. There is a continued need to include a range of behavioral, cognitive, and physiological measures in subsequent investigations.

A recent reviewer (Pallone, 1988) has noted the absence of systematic research to establish precise linkages between alcohol and offending behaviors. In particular, previous studies have relied on self-reports of the offender (or victim), with few accounts based on laboratory assessments of criminogenic substance use/abuse. The absence of "biochemically determined neuropsychological sequelae to the use and abuse of...dangerous substances" (Pallone, 1988) has been a retardant to progress in the field. Laboratory assays, collected nearer to the occurrence of offending behavior, would help to compensate for the limitations of self-reports, which usually occur long after the offense event. The use of such immunoassays has produced recent estimates that 50% of arrestees have used alcohol/other drugs before their apprehension.

Conclusions

In conclusion, current research has not yet produced data to permit reliable estimates about the percentages of criminal offenses committed by intoxicated persons. Furthermore, the research does not permit differential conclusions about which substances accelerate which offending behaviors. The focus of inquiry from sociology, psychology, and criminology may require additional contributions from biochemistry and neuropsychopharmacology.

3

Alcohol Education and Interventions

The precise nature of the relationship between offending and alcohol abuse remains unknown. Attempts have been made, however, to address the problem of intoxicated offenders by provision of alternatives to custodial care. The development of AECs as a secondary intervention procedure has been based on change attempts via the provision of information on alcohol and abstinence/controlled drinking goals. At a theoretical level, a decline in the prominence of the medical model, toward acceptance of social learning concepts, has driven practical applications such as AECs for offenders with drinking problems.

Although AECs have been expanded across statutory and nonstatutory agencies, criticism has been leveled that they have produced few long term benefits. As controlled systematic research has not yet been achieved, this cannot be assessed. Thus, AECs have been implemented without much knowledge of their effectiveness, leading to doubt and uncertainty for the staff who implement them. In addition, data-based justification of AECs to funding and referral agencies as an effective use of resources has been very limited.

The Alcohol/Offending Interface

While the precise nature of the relationship between alcohol and offending behaviors has remained unclear, there is overwhelming support for such a link (Greenberg, 1982; McGuire & Priestley, 1985; Pernanen, 1982). Despite methodological inadequacies of demographic and epidemiological surveys and serious design problems of experimental/clinical interventions, however, the climate for further empirical enquiry in this field has remained hopeful during the 1980s (Collins, 1982).

Paradoxically, this optimism has persisted despite an accumulation of evidence from the literature on offending behavior that most interventions with this population have not been successful (Blackburn, 1980). Similarly, in the alcohol field, the evidence for long term maintenance of therapeutic gains for offender/clients has been inconclusive (Hershon et al., 1974). This paucity of rigorous research studies to examine the interface between alcohol and offending behaviors in client populations has contributed to conditions of uncertainty among researchers, fieldworkers, and offender/clients. Nonetheless, fieldwork practice of educational or rehabilitative interventions with offender/clients has flourished, usually in the conspicuous absence of any supporting data.

Several explanations are possible for the continued optimism and expansion of forensic services to include alcohol/offending interventions (e.g., AECs) for clients. First, there have been legislative and legal changes both in the United States and Western Europe, which have increased the probabilities of certain court disposals (McGuire & Priestley, 1985). This may have generated the climate in which the range of court disposals for offender/clients has been expanded. Second, statutory fieldworkers have continued their involvement in the service provision of such interventions. Third, the expansion of nonstatutory alcohol/addictions agencies, at least in the United Kingdom, has increased the range of sentencing disposals available to the courts (Tether & Robinson, 1986). Fourth, the general dominant social ethos for behavior change of individual offenders, rather than of social systems (Staulcup et al., 1979), has continued in the United Kingdom and United States. Moreover, although there have been some exceptions, (e.g., Scandinavia), this trend also has been dominant in other Western European countries (Nilson-Giebel, 1980). In summary, whereas the range of court sentencing options may have been expanded, *the focus of interventions generally has remained on individual offender/clients and not on system change.*

In recent years, knowledge about the alcohol/offending interface has reflected a trend toward the study of juveniles and young adults rather than older adult offenders. This may reflect a more general trend in the alcohol field that has focused on "secondary prevention" and "health promotion" attempts with younger client populations (Tether & Robinson, 1985). It has been concomitant with a continued forensic interest in remedial interventions with younger offender/clients. Paradoxically, however, while fieldwork practice with juveniles and young adults with alcohol problems may have increased, this has not always been reflected in research studies (Vingilis, 1981). Evidently, the relationship between nonproblem drinking, problem drinking, detection, and subsequent conviction is extremely complex and is subject to systematic bias in both reporting and recording (Pernanen, 1982). Many studies have not contained adequate control groups and have been flawed by unresolved methodological problems; the use of the term "alcohol-related," for example, may be misleading in consideration of the role of alcohol in criminal behavior, as offense titles do not always reflect intoxication at the time of the offense (Vingilis, 1981).

Although limited by criticisms of reliability and validity, there have been several attempts to investigate the link between alcohol and offending behavior among incarcerated populations of offenders (Greenberg, 1982). Questionnaire and interview studies among this population have indicated that between 55% and 85% of offender/clients acknowledge an involvement of alcohol in their offense behaviors. Moreover, part of the initiative for secondary intervention attempts with juvenile and young adult offenders has resulted from surveys among this population (Heather, 1981, 1982; Miller & Welte, 1987). Acknowledgment of the limitations of abstinence goals among a population of young offender/clients (who have high probabilities for subsequent drinking and intoxication) has increased the interest in behavioral interventions based on controlled drinking goals (Heather, 1981; Heather & Robertson, 1983a).

Forensic studies of the alcohol/offending interface have been supplemented in more recent years by generic, rather than specialist, perspectives (Hawkins, 1982). In a field where the body of knowledge in general has been established by highly specialist participants, this "new genericism" has been invaluable in the understanding of the nexus between delinquent/nondelinquent behavior and problem/nonproblem drinking patterns. The developmental perspective has been of particular relevance (Hawkins, 1982; Kandel, 1980).

The link between alcohol and offending behaviors seems to have transcended cultural and national boundaries, especially with regard to drinking and subsequent intoxication among adolescents and young adults. Most demographic and epidemiological surveys have indicated clear trends in this population of drinkers (Ahlstrom, 1985). In contrast, however, intervention attempts based on scientific data-based approaches to resolve alcohol problems among this population of offender/clients have been restricted to a few countries, specifically North America, the United Kingdom, and in some Scandinavian countries (i.e., Sweden, Denmark, Norway). Moreover, although there have been some accounts of quasi-experimental studies at the alcohol-offending interface (Lenke, 1982), most studies in this field have been restricted to descriptive statistics or intervention attempts in the absence of control groups. Several recent reviews have emphasized the need for robust experimental studies with methodological rigor, especially with adequate controls (Blackburn, 1980; Greenberg, 1982; Hudson, 1977; Pernanen, 1982). In sum, despite much progress in the field in the 1980s, where fieldwork has flourished scientific analysis has floundered.

Legal Systems and State Legislation

Forensic research on offender/clients brought before United Kingdom courts was started at the beginning of the 1970s. Several descriptive surveys have been completed, each of which has stated a need for the expansion of court-based remedial-rehabilitative interventions (Gath et al., 1968; Hawker & Stevenson, 1984; Out of Court, 1982). These surveys have taken samples of offenders appearing before courts and have used epidemiological data (based on client interviews) and outcome data (based on court sentencing patterns) to argue for a wider range of services available to the judiciary. Such data have been used as a proposal to remove the offender/client from the legal arena into a medical/psychiatric context. Thus, while there has been recognition that services offered to offenders with alcohol problems have been inadequate, one conclusion of this position has been the renewed argument for more medical/psychiatric resources (Gath et al., 1968).

This "medicalization" of the offender/client with alcohol problems has remained a contentious topic among many service agencies and their representatives. There have been wide cross-national differences in this area; in the United States there has been a long history of alcohol/offending problems considered as an "illness" (Mitchell, 1971) and there is ample evidence that such beliefs have persisted (Miller, 1987a). In contrast, in the United Kingdom there has been a shift of opinion, such that demedicalization of alcohol/offending problems has continued (Heather & Robertson, 1983a); the dominant contemporary United Kingdom ethos is probably closer to social learning theory than the medical model (Orford, 1986).

Notwithstanding these national and cultural differences, the proposition of court-based interventions based on prior interviewing and assessment is not novel. Such a scheme was proposed as early as 1974 in the United Kingdom, based on a prospective study using diagnostic/problem assessment (Hershon et al., 1974). Echoing previous reports, the study noted constancy of the problems for "disposal" produced by offender/clients with an overlay of problem drinking. Other subsequent reports (Hamilton, 1976; Hamilton, Griffiths, Ritson, & Aikens, 1977) extended this proposal to argue for additional medical resources, including the establishment of detoxification services. Ironically, the failure to establish a national network of detoxification services in the United Kingdom, based on the original model, may have contributed to the increased usage of alternative, nonmedical disposals for offenders with alcohol problems (McGuire & Priestley, 1985).

This shift of emphasis in the United Kingdom to nonlegal and nonmedical interventions has been assisted by the ascendency of other nonstatutory agencies not involved specifically in alcohol services. Some, for example, have argued for the provision of services for offenders with alcohol problems to be provided by social agencies and not from the courts (Out of Court, 1982). This lobby has been particularly active in highlighting the needs of juvenile and young adult offenders who have multiple problems, often including substance abuse, chronic unemployment, and homelessness. In addition, there has been a parallel interest in the development of more creative disposal policies, for example, based on imaginative use of probation sentencing (Priestley et al., 1984). In the United Kingdom, these developments have established a context for the potential promotion of a wider range of interventions with offenders, including the provision of AECs.

Does Alcohol Education Work?

The provision of AECs for offenders with alcohol problems was first established in Scotland in 1981 (Robertson & Heather, 1982a). This Scottish AEC initially was based on a behavioral rationale. Parallel developments of AECs in England, however, were based on the proposition that the provision of information about alcohol would bring about subsequent behavior change in individuals. Since their inception, these two types of service delivery have continued to develop in the United Kingdom on quite separate trajectories.

Reviewers of the literature on alcohol education have indicated that the same premise (i.e., that provision of information alone will produce behavior change) has dominated the field since the late 1960s. A key review paper (while noting the lack of objectives, absence of clear philosophy and lack of outcome research) still defined the essence of alcohol education as the provision of information to improve decision-making. Moreover, within the United States, there has been a major policy initiative to teach adaptive drinking patterns among juveniles and young adults, with a particular emphasis on alcohol education in schools (Freeman & Scott, 1966; Unterberg & Di Ciccio, 1968).

More recently, these programs have received widespread criticism because of a failure to make explicit the underlying educational assumptions. In addition, few tests have been made of program effectiveness or cost benefits (Goodstadt, 1978). There has also been criticism of the model based on provision of knowledge to influence subsequent health behavior; there is scant evidence for this proposition, and evidently no cause-effect relationship exists. Similar criticisms have been made of the supposed relationship between attitudes, values, and behavior: many alcohol education initiatives have been based on the premise that adaptive behavior change will result from values clarification or attitude change (Goodstadt, 1978; Staulcup et al., 1979). The evidence for this proposition, however, has been conspicuous by its absence.

Most alcohol education initiatives have continued to focus on modification of knowledge, attitudes, beliefs, and values of individual drinkers. This approach has been consistent with socialization theory, based on the premise that faulty learning (i.e., problem drinking) can be corrected by new learning or resocialization experiences. More recently, there has been a shift of focus in the United States and the United Kingdom away from "primary prevention" (services directed to reduce the incidence/prevalence of alcohol misuse) toward "secondary prevention" (early intervention with persons who already have alcohol problems).

Despite this shift to strategies that are more amenable to the use of robust experimental designs (e.g., control groups), however, evaluation attempts have been sparse. None of 21 alcohol education projects reviewed in 1979 was based on a strong experimental design, and none was able to demonstrate any links between knowledge/attitude changes and subsequent drinking behavior (Staulcup et al., 1979). Moreover, later reviews have suggested that alcohol/other drug education programs may *increase* use of these substances and increase problem incidence among some client populations (Kinder et al., 1980). An increase in factual knowledge alone is insufficient to change attitudes and behavior; indeed, in isolation it may increase the possibility of substance abuse.

This continued provision of "primary" and "secondary" alcohol education programs, without supportive data, has been viewed as a response to a crisis in the field. Several sets of recommendations for subsequent intervention attempts have been provided. These have included the need for descriptions of subjects/methods, basic experimental procedures, appropriate statistics, and outcome measures on attitudes, knowledge, behavior, and other adequate measures (Kinder et al., 1980). Other reviewers have stated the need for client-specific programs, drinking options, values-clarification, and paraprofessional presenters (Engs, 1982).

Moreover, there has been wider recognition that to enable change in the behavior of drinkers, program contents should confront behavioral not attitudinal themes;

instructions for achievement of the desired change in behavior should be clear, explicit, and accessible to the target audience (Grant, 1982).

This need to focus on behavioral themes to achieve behavioral goals has provided a shift of impetus in the field of alcohol education. A recent review has traced the history of alcohol/drug education through the four phases of moral objection, fear approaches, objective facts, and values clarification and decision making (Flay & Sobell, 1983). It concluded that prevention programs should focus on skills acquisition by client groups, in order to reduce or ameliorate substance abuse problems. It is precisely this shift toward the achievement of behavior change, via skills acquisition, that has provided the impetus for the establishment and subsequent controlled evaluation of AECs in Scotland.

Offending Behavior: Change Attempts

An inspection of the literature on achievement of behavior change in offender/clients might lead to the conclusion that "nothing works." In the 1970s this was a common perspective in United Kingdom social work. Moreover, there is some evidence that apprehension itself by service agencies creates a worse outcome with juveniles than nonapprehension. Two researchers have suggested that apprehension of young adult and juvenile offenders did not produce a "deterrent" effect; furthermore, they concluded that apprehension by police and subsequent court interventions encouraged further delinquent/offending behaviors (Gold, 1969; Gold & Williams, 1969). Moreover, reviews of correctional outcome have suggested equivocal findings of a pervasive lack of methodological rigor, (e.g., inadequate design, poor statistical analyses, absence of controls) and sparse evidence for the efficacy of interventions (Bailey, 1966; Davidson & Seidman, 1974). In addition, another reviewer has challenged the general assumption of superior effectiveness of behavioral interventions in noninstitutionalized settings (Blackburn, 1980).

Despite questions raised by these findings, this uncertain climate of doubt and reappraisal has set the conditions for a renewed interest in the evaluation of specific interventions with well-defined offender/client populations. There has been a focus on matching clients with particular characteristics to individual or group interventions (Blomqvist & Holmberg, 1988; Glaser, 1980). It has been based on an interest in the development of adaptive new behaviors in offender/clients.

Several studies based on skills acquisition have suggested that highly specific intervention programs may offer the most promising approach for further investment of resources. The acquisition of interaction skills, for example, via the provision of social skills training, has demonstrated meaningful improvements at follow-up that are both reliable and durable (Spence, 1979; Spence & Marzillier, 1979, 1981). Thus, despite the overwhelming evidence both from the United States and the United Kingdom, that most intervention procedures do not work (Feldman, 1976; Hood & Sparks, 1970), there is some optimism about highly specific interventions based on careful matching with highly specific and carefully selected offender/clients.

Alcohol Education Courses for Court-Ordered Individuals

Since 1981 there have been two parallel developments of AECs for individuals with alcohol problems court-ordered for interventions. These two initiatives have been developed independently in England and Scotland. In England, the initiative and subsequent impetus for the development of these services was based on an increasing use of probation-based sentencing in the early 1980s. After the initial AECs in England during 1981 and 1982, these courses flourished within probation services, sometimes in liaison with local nonstatutory alcohol agencies (i.e., Councils on Alcohol). Despite a steady increase in this type of service provision for offenders with drinking problems, however, no systematic controlled evaluation of effectiveness has occurred in English probation services. Nonetheless, some early reports with descriptive statistics and outcome data on drinking/offending behaviors have suggested promising results (Godfrey & Leahy, 1986; Menary, 1986; Singer, 1983).

A recent review of the development of AECs in United Kingdom services suggested that they have developed rapidly since 1981. This review of 20 agencies (Baldwin & Heather, 1987) indicated that at least 1,750 offenders had completed an AEC; moreover, it indicated an interest (if not an active commitment) by service agents to collect follow-up data on drinking/offending behaviors. Although these 20 agencies had completed more than 240 AECs in 6 years, no data on effectiveness were available.

A striking finding of this review was the apparent similarity of AECs in different geographical locations. While these services had been developed ad hoc without a design template, most AECs included common ingredients (e.g., films, handouts, group exercises). The linking theme, however, was a reliance on the provision of information, facts, and knowledge about alcohol, irrespective of their geographical location or their date in the chronological sequence of national service development.

Despite the inclusion of some ingredients to promote drinking behavior change (e.g., drink diaries), most English AECs appear to have adhered to knowledge/ attitudes ingredients, to the exclusion of explicit behavioral themes. A second review of AEC services in the United Kingdom (Gamba et al., 1989) has reported similar descriptive data, confirming earlier trends.

An absence of outcome data on AEC effectiveness has continued in England since the inception of these services. In Scotland, however, the first controlled evaluation of AECs was started in 1985. This was established and maintained to evaluate AEC services for individuals court-ordered for interventions with alcohol problems. These courses have shared many common features with the English AEC model (e.g., a focus on controlled drinking goals, 12 hours duration, six weekly sessions, alcohol information/facts, multimodal presentation, service uptake by nonstatutory agencies). In addition, AECs have contained many of the same components as programs for behavioral self-control training (Miller, 1987a).

Other features have been quite different, including use of "deferred sentencing" instead of probation orders, focus on behavioral change of drinking/offending patterns via skills acquisition, an explicit commitment to evaluation, and time-limited contracting with agencies to provide services. These modifications have occurred as a specific response to an attempt to establish data-based court services for juvenile and young adult offenders with drink problems (Baldwin, Ford, & Heather, 1987; Baldwin, Ford, Heather, & Braggins, 1987).

Implementation Problems with Court-Ordered Interventions

The successful establishment and maintenance of a network of AECs for individuals with alcohol problems, court-ordered for intervention, has been achieved throughout the United Kingdom since 1981. Despite this rapid development of service provision, however, several problems remain unresolved. First, many service agencies have reported persistent difficulties related to funding, staffing, system support, and recognition for their interventions with offender/clients (Baldwin & Heather, 1987). To establish these services, many agents (probation officers, social workers, psychologists) have been required to invest their own time and resources to ensure program survival. This may be related to the perceived low status of offenders within society and a possible "halo effect" for those staff who work with them.

Certainly, there is a pervasive dogma that asserts that offenders with drinking problems make active choices about their life styles and are entirely responsible for their own personal and social circumstances. This set of societal beliefs, attitudes, and behaviors can make working with offenders who have drinking problems unattractive, and ultimately unrewarding for staff, because of the low success rates and the effects of active devaluation. Moreover, there is continued, unresolved debate about the "status" of offenders with drinking problems within the court system. Historically, there have been shifts away from an illness/disease perspective toward an understanding based on social learning theory (Miller, 1987b; Stumphauzer, 1986). The conceptual shift has been long overdue, and has assisted in the development of a range of intervention programs for people with drinking problems.

Nonetheless, the demise of illness/disease models may have produced secondary effects; in particular the perceived focus of responsibility for drinking/offending problems has shifted back to the individual offender. This, combined with twin political administrations during the 1980s in the United Kingdom and United States, may have contributed to a more punitive ethos within the courts, based on a strong "law and order" philosophy. This effect may have been compounded by continued confusion about alcohol and "drugs."

Not only are there conflicting and inconsistent attitudes and behaviors by adults about their own drug use, but alcohol is generally not viewed as a drug (Hawkins, 1982). The recent focus of attention and funding on "drugs" (sic) may have contributed to the drain of resources from alcohol programs.

Second, there have been genuine conflicts for court officials and administration staff who have supported court-based interventions for offenders with drink problems. For example, the judiciary are the focus of a dilemma between "punishment" and "rehabilitation" of offender/clients. A pervasive law-and-order ethos inevitably will reduce the probability of use of nonretributive sentencing options. Moreover, in a legal system where the judiciary has been accountable to the public and must seek reelection, they will err on the side of caution and minimize "risky" sentencing options that "let the offender of the hook." Also, additional cultural effects may have influenced this system designed to maintain the status quo; certainly within the Scots culture, there is an indigenous conservatism, rooted in a traditional scepticism that awaits the proof of a method before trying it (Balfour-Sclare, 1985). There are associated practical problems with time and resources; in overcrowded courts that process hundreds of cases in a week, the additional work involved in processing referrals and reports for alternative sentencing options may deter court officials from supporting such schemes.

Third, chronic recruitment problems have contributed to the nonevaluation of AECs, despite their widespread adoption as court-ordered interventions in the United Kingdom. Some AECs have been discontinued, not simply because of lack of staffing or funding but because of insufficient referrals from courts (Gamba et al., 1989; Warden, 1986). The establishment of an adequate base rate of referrals has been problematic for many AEC services in the United Kingdom, although the use of probation orders in England (rather than deferred sentencing options in Scotland) may have increased referral rates (McLoone, Oulds & Morris, 1987).

Given the prevalence of offenders who commit crime while intoxicated, it is paradoxical that court-based intervention programs have received meager support within the judicial system. Some possible explanatory factors include court workloads, cultural conservatism, insufficient data on effectiveness, and a pervasive "law-and-order" ethos both from the public and in the courts. Another factor, however, has been related specifically to the adoption of controlled drinking programs. Other reviews have noted the difficulty of recruiting clients for such programs in the United States (Miller, 1987b) and in Scotland (Cameron & Spence, 1976). The precise reasons for this remain unknown. Probable explanations, no doubt, relate to cultural conservatism, conflict of interest, suspicion of newness, and system reactance.

Summary

The provision of AECs for individual offenders court-ordered for interventions with alcohol problems has been a major development in United Kingdom forensic service provision. It has broadened the narrow range of intervention options beyond referrals to single agencies for abstinence programs (Young & Lawson, 1985). The approach has offered the extension of such service provision beyond alcohol specialists to generic workers, who have assisted offenders to acquire skills to reduce probabilities of reoffending (e.g., Remington & Remington, 1987).

4

Alcohol Education Courses

Original Alcohol Education Course Package—1981

It has been notoriously difficult to recruit clients most likely to benefit from reduced drinking behavior change programs. In particular, younger clients with problems of minor or moderate severity may not perceive themselves as requiring assistance because they have not been aware of alcohol-related problems (Leathar, 1978). Despite the lack of clarity about the relationship between drinking and offending, a subgroup of young offenders has been identified whose drinking patterns were characterized by other problems such as morning drinking and memory blackouts (Heather, 1981, 1982). Irrespective of the presence or absence of a *causal* link with offending behaviors, intervention with this subgroup would be justifiable to ameliorate the alcohol-related problems.

The decision to intervene with young offenders has raised the question about the optimum level of prevention for this group. The knowledge that some alcohol (or other drug) education programs have *increased* the probability of subsequent usage has sensitized some drug educators to modify their approach (Kinder et al., 1980). With some exceptions, however, most of these programs concentrated on information provision, not skills acquisition, as the main component of behavior change. Such studies may have been flawed by their design inadequacy, which restricted program contents to nonpotent ingredients. The alcohol/other drug education literature has suggested that the evidence for the efficacy of "secondary prevention" is greater than the evidence for "primary prevention" initiatives, although evidence for both is scant (Kinder et al., 1980). One study of alcohol education with small group discussions showed particularly promising results (Williams, Di Ciccio, & Unterberger, 1968).

Evidence from other related research has suggested that "secondary prevention" programs using self-help manuals and minimal therapist contact have provided an effective means of change for problem drinkers (Heather & Robertson, 1981; Miller & Taylor, 1980). Combinations of these two areas of research provided the impetus for the preliminary AEC in Tayside, Scotland. Specifically, this program was based both on flexible small group discussions and didactic behaviorally based interventions.

Candidates for the AEC were selected from the Sheriff courts in Dundee with the assistance of the Social Work Department. The court procedure ensured that offender/clients whose offenses were "alcohol-related" were offered an opportunity to attend an AEC via a probation order. Offenders were given a brief interview by a research psychologist to determine previous and current levels of drinking, attitudes to drinking, and patterns of offending. Specific selection criteria were used to filter potential clients into an AEC group. These criteria required a "yes" answer to at least one of three questions:

1. "Would you say you had a drink problem?" or
2. "Are you worried about your drinking?" or
3. "Do you think you would get into less trouble if you didn't drink so much?"

or, that more than half of all previous offenses were committed while intoxicated. Candidates who answered affirmatively and agreed to work on their drinking were recommended for a probation order of 12 months to attend an AEC.

Ethical Considerations

The use of interventions with detained (or incarcerated) offenders has raised the question of ethical problems, and possible conflicts of interest between research/clinical needs and the needs of offender/clients. Strong arguments have been generated against compulsory interventions with offender/client populations (Newman, 1971; Room, 1980; Szasz, 1963). Such arguments have been based on the consideration of the right not to be treated. The counter argument has been based on a recognition that some at-risk individuals have not acquired the necessary information or skills to make informed choices: intervention with such persons may be justified if agents genuinely act "in the person's best interests."

Provision of AECs for offender/clients was based on three principles to address these ethical themes:

1. serious attempts were made to evaluate efficacy of interventions
2. interventions did not involve incarceration and/or removal of personal liberty
3. candidates were free to decline AEC participation, without sanctions or punishment greater than those existing before the establishment of the AECs

In addition, candidates were selected if they were: (a) under 25 years old, (b) showing no signs of severe alcohol dependence (SADQ ≤ 35), and (c) not showing signs of psychiatric morbidity (assessed by interview team).

With some exceptions (Pattison, 1976), for the younger, male drinker a moderate/controlled drinking goal may be the "treatment of choice" (Heather & Robertson, 1981). Indeed, for some young people, abstinence goals may be associated with a higher probability of subsequent relapse (Orford, 1973). In addition, for persons with moderate alcohol problems, abstinence goals may be associated with higher consumption of alcohol in the short-term (Sanchez-Craig, 1980). Offender/clients with "serious levels of dependence" were excluded from the AECs and candidates were offered a controlled drinking goal.

Contents of the Alcohol Education Course

The AEC was designed to run for six weekly sessions, each lasting 90 minutes. The AEC was based on a self-help manual given to each participant. Sessions included didactic teaching methods about alcohol knowledge as well as group discussions about individual topics. AEC contents included:

SESSION ONE: INTRODUCTION

—film showing basic facts about alcohol
—fill in "reason for drinking" questionnaire and discuss "pros and cons" of each session

SESSION TWO: MATHEMATICS OF INTOXICATION

—use of slides and other aids to provide basic information about alcohol drinking
—blood alcohol concentration (BAC) levels
—strength of drinks
—rate of absorption of alcohol in relation to food, weight, and time
—behavior likely at different BAC levels
—causes of "passing out"
—introduction to self-monitoring
—use of charts to calculate BAC levels
—plan BAC levels for different drinking situations in next week and calculate intake accordingly
—presentation of "drinking rules"

SESSION THREE: WHY DO I DO AS I DO?

—individual functional analysis (completed by participants with help in their own manual), e.g., "where, when, how, with whom?" in relation to their own drinking
—definition of "high-risk" circumstances for each individual
—formulation and writing-down of individualized drinking rules for each participant

SESSION FOUR: SURVIVAL AIDS

—discussion of individual drinking records for past week and discussion of obstacles to moderate drinking in relation to the previous week's analysis
—discussions and role-playing of potential risky situations

Session Five: Problem-Solving Training and Alternative Activities

—presentation of techniques for dealing with problems—especially those of boredom and unemployment
—"brainstorming" session about alternatives to drinking and the formulation of individual strategies for this, written in the manual

Session Six: Review

—summary of last 5 weeks' work
—facts about "alcohol dependence" and alcohol problems
—discussion with young "recovered alcoholics" (Robertson & Heather, 1982a).

Preliminary Findings

Ten offender/clients completed the first AEC in Tayside. AECs were discontinued, however, because of the difficulty in obtaining sufficient referrals from the courts. Neither outcome data nor follow-up data were collected on these subjects as part of the AEC study, although a subsequent attempt has been made to follow-up this cohort (Baldwin, Lawson & Mooney, 1991).

These initial results confirmed it was possible to implement a service to the courts based on AEC attendance by young offender/clients. Although process, outcome, and follow-up data were not collected, subjective measures had suggested that AEC members had not reoffended during the course. Nonetheless, certain "systems" problems had persisted throughout, and remained unresolved. These included:

1. failure to generate sufficient referrals for AEC candidates from the courts
2. noninvolvement of other service staff (e.g., social workers)
3. failure to collect data on efficacy of AECs

In combination, these factors prevented further development, and the service was discontinued after the initial AEC in 1981, 5 years after the first exploratory discussions in 1976 to establish this court service in Tayside.

Controlled Drinking/Minimal Interventions

The choice of intervention goals with people who have drinking problems has been the subject of much debate. Historically, there has been much pressure to direct clients toward abstinence goals within a treatment ethos with a strong moral background. Until the 1960s, intervention goals other than abstinence were uncommon or remained unreported/unpublished. Publication of the seminal study of heavy drinkers who had achieved controlled drinking (Davies, 1962) demonstrated that nonabstinent goals might be appropriate for some client populations. Many other studies have since demonstrated that clients can achieve controlled drinking goals (Heather & Robertson, 1983a; Pattison, 1976). These observations have been based on experimental research (Sobell & Sobell; 1973, 1976), survey observations (Bailey & Tennant, 1967), and controlled drinking groups (Bruun, 1966).

Inconsistent usage of terms such as "controlled drinking" has limited comparisons between studies; definitions of a "controlled drinker" have been neither uniform nor precise. A review of the usage of nonabstinent drinking goals with intervention programs (Pattison, 1976) suggested that terms such as "social drinking" be discarded in favor of the more operationally accurate "attenuated drinking." Other work has suggested that controlled/attenuated drinking goals may be the "treatment of choice" with specific client groups. Moreover, abstinence goals may produce specific problems for some clients, including impossible rehabilitation targets, failure to join or complete intervention programs, punishment of nonabstinent clients, failure to appreciate other goals achieved by drinkers, marginalization of other intervention goals, "victim-blaming" of nonabstinent clients, and deemphasis of other nonabstinent intervention goals (Pattison, 1976). Several studies have stated the need for a differential assessment process, leading to individualized intervention programs with individualized goals.

More recent research has confirmed the validity of establishing behavior change programs for problem drinkers in noninstitutional settings. Many of these studies have demonstrated the benefits of nonabstinent drinking goals for groups of clients in local neighborhood settings (Vogler, Weissbach, Compton, & Martin, 1977). Recognition of problem drinking as "a reversible behavioural disorder rather than an irreversible disease" (Heather & Robertson, 1983b) has shifted the focus of attention to the establishment of controlled drinking/nonabstinent goals in intervention programs. This has been of particular salience to behavior change agents working with young client populations who have not yet developed serious alcohol problems. Thus, while abstinence goals have continued to be viewed as the optimum strategy for people with chronic drinking problems, controlled/attenuated drinking goals often have been viewed as the "treatment of choice" with younger male drinkers who have not developed a serious alcohol problem (Heather & Robertson, 1983a).

Optimal application of controlled drinking methods may relate to interventions with early-stage problem drinkers who would otherwise be deterred from seeking assistance by the prospect of abstinence goals (Miller, 1983b; Sobell & Sobell, 1982). A common finding in this area has been that intensive treatments have been no more effective than various forms of "minimal interventions" (Miller, 1978; Miller & Taylor, 1980; Miller, Taylor & West, 1980; Vogler et al., 1977). Other authors similarly have reported no overall differences between intensive and minimal interventions, despite some evidence for greater improvements with intensive interventions among clients with more severe problems (Orford, Oppenheimer, & Edwards, 1976). In contrast, more recent studies (Robertson et al., 1986) reported greater effectiveness of intensive controlled drinking treatments than for minimal interventions (based on assessment and advice only). The effective component of "minimal interventions" may have been the self-help manuals, based on behavioral principles. More recently one researcher has suggested that sequencing of materials (i.e., information/skills teaching) may impact on outcome (Savage, 1988).

Minimal Interventions

An intervention may be considered "minimal" if it entails less professional time or resources than typically involved in group (or individual) face-to-face interventions (Heather, 1986a). They may include the use of self-help manuals, with or without therapist/counsellor involvement. One reason for increased professional interest in minimal interventions (including the use of self-help manuals or "bibliotherapy") has been the recognition that interventions with problem drinking may be selected from a "continuum of intensity."

Specifically, the distinction between "education" and "treatment" has become blurred with greater focus on matching clients to interventions. Other minimal interventions have included self-help manuals, audio tapes, video tapes, postal contact, and telephone reporting. Another major factor has been the need to develop more cost-effective interventions for larger client populations that require service provision, despite diminishing resources.

Other advantages of minimal interventions include the reduced probability of iatrogenic effects of medicalized treatments and the low probability of secondary handicapping or stigmatization from unnecessary labeling. In addition, self-help approaches (e.g., manuals) have been developed within the framework of the scientifically based principles of self-management theory (Karoly & Kanfer, 1982; Thoreson & Mahoney, 1974). This behavioral technology has provided the empirical framework for the development of self-help materials.

The demise of disease theories of alcohol has increased the recognition that early-stage problem drinkers provide a legitimate target for intervention attempts (Heather, 1986b; Heather & Robertson, 1983a, b). In particular, this paradigm shift has prompted an increased interest in service provision based on "secondary prevention" (i.e., nonchronic client populations who have already developed some alcohol problems). The use of minimal interventions also has been consistent with the recognition that abstinence goals may be counterproductive with early-stage problem drinkers (Sanchez-Craig, 1980).

Given the array of clients, problems, and interventions, a need to establish a rational basis for assignment of clients to interventions has remained paramount (Blomqvist & Holmberg, 1988). This has been particularly salient in interventions with offenders, where few treatment matching attempts have been established. Nonetheless, most interventions with offender/clients (McGuire & Priestley, 1985) have been applied in the absence of a direct focus on program contents, group selection, or client-specific materials (Blackburn, 1980).

One theoretician has proposed that the intensity of an intervention required will be determined by the stage of change previously reached by the client (Prochaska & Di Clemente, 1982). The challenge for practitioners, therefore, has been to match interventions with the stage of change of clients, to maximize (a) cost effectiveness,

(b) probability of success, and (c) probability of maintenance of therapeutic gains. The application of minimal interventions to young offenders in small groups has been one low-cost attempt to promote therapeutic gains with an at-risk client population.

National Context of Alcohol Educations Courses

Since 1979, development of AECs has continued without systematic attempts at coordination, monitoring, or evaluation. In England and Wales, most AECs have been developed in probation services, often initiated by individual practitioners with a special interest in alcohol and offending. In Scotland, until 1985 there were no attempts at systematic evaluation of effectiveness of AECs, despite some investments from several social work departments. The overall situation in the United Kingdom until 1985 was of extensive, haphazard, service provision but without planning or evaluation. Examination of United Kingdom services has suggested two main origins of AECs: Corby (England) and Dundee (Scotland).

England, Northern Ireland, and Wales

The development of AECs has not been well documented, although some inhouse publications were completed by several social work/probation departments. The first published account of the development of AECs was a study of the Corby Alcohol Therapy Group (NPS, 1982). The report was a service-based descriptive account of the "Alcohol Therapy Group" from 1979 to 1981. As the name suggests, the alcohol therapy group was provided as a rehabilitative option for clients with drinking-related offending behaviors. This report offered descriptive accounts of the ATG contents with supplementary demographic material about offenders who had attended the ATG. An initial before/after evaluation was planned; reconviction rates were compared for 12 months preceding and following the first 40 cases. A reduction from 1.77 to 1.08 offenses per year was reported.

The second report on the development of AEC services was based on similar work completed in Coventry (Bailey & Purser, 1982). The work extended the original Corby model to develop a court-based Alcohol Education Group service. This was a probation service initiative, which subsequently was incorporated into the nonstatutory local Council on Alcohol. Similar to Corby, the initiative started with several "key people" who developed the concept of alcohol education according to a personal philosophy. Both projects were characterized by low funding, minimal staffing, no resources, minimal planning, and no evaluation.

The first attempt at even minimal evaluation was based on the Alcohol Study Group in Berkshire (Singer, 1983). The ASG was similar to the Coventry AEG model with six weekly sessions of alcohol education/information designed to "educate participants about the damage alcohol can cause" (Singer, 1983). The ASG service was court-based and operated by the Probation Service.

A before/after evaluation attempt was based on measurement of offending rates. At 12 month follow-up, 11 offenders from a pool of 33 had reoffended (33.3%); those offenders completing the ASG had a reconviction rate of 24%, and those who dropped out had a reconviction rate of 62.5%. Other improvements were noted, including increased alcohol knowledge, more adaptive attitudes to drinking, and reduced intake of volume alcohol at follow-up (Singer, 1983).

The Berkshire ASG project has remained the best documented account of alcohol education work with offenders in England, Wales, or Northern Ireland. Despite the evaluation attempt, however, the generalizability of the results of this study have been restricted by design limitations. Specifically, the study was based on a relatively weak pretest/posttest design and did not include a control group. Thus, although the ASG report provided a useful account of process variables in alcohol education initiatives with offenders (e.g., demographic information, dropout rates, subjective effectiveness data), the potency of the project was severely limited by key methodological flaws.

More recently, the Berkshire model has been reduplicated in Somerset, with some amendments to the original ASG course contents (Menary, 1986). The Somerset Alcohol Education Course (AEC) has reworked many ingredients of previous alcohol education initiatives. It has also included more behavioral components, however, including one skills teaching session. The AEC has been developed according to a structure of alcohol information and behavioral self-monitoring. Although the initial report has not included data on effectiveness, an evaluation project was planned for 1988/89. This evaluation included follow-up data of offenders who had completed an AEC but the experimental design did not include control groups.

Another study has reported preliminary findings from alcohol education programs (AEPs) in Devon (Godfrey & Leahy, 1986). The report provided initial findings for the first four AEPs completed during 1984/85. Some data were reported for 54 offenders, 30 of whom had completed an AEP. Specifically, increases of between 25% and 90% in alcohol knowledge was reported, 32% cut down their drinking to a level within their personal targets, and 36% reduced their overall consumption. Although this study did not include a control group, modest improvements were reported for offenders who completed an AEP. The data on effectiveness indicated "a slightly lower reconviction rate for compulsory attenders" (Godfrey & Leahy, 1986).

Scotland

The original AEC study in Scotland was based on a group of 10 offenders who completed a course in 1981, although no formal evaluation was planned and no follow-up data were available (Robertson & Heather, 1982a). The AEC was based on information about alcohol and some behavioral methods for reducing drinking/offending. The AEC court service was not continued because of problems with system maintenance. This work was terminated in Dundee in 1982.

Despite discontinuation of this service in Dundee, the same AEC model was transferred to Forfar (Angus) during 1981. A similar service was established by a senior social worker to provide a referral/AEC service in the Sheriff (High) courts. Offender/clients with alcohol-related offending behaviors have attended an AEC as a condition of a probation order (Baldwin et al., 1987; Baldwin, Ford, Heather & Braggins, 1987). Despite the achievement of 18 AECs since 1981, however, no systematic follow-up has been completed and data on effectiveness have not been collected. One descriptive study has been completed, however, (Ward & Baldwin, 1990).

Another service in Dumbarton has reported findings for follow-ups of individual offenders with alcohol problems (Collins & Tate, 1988; Tate, 1985). Although the agency has not provided AECs for offender/clients, an individual counseling service has been offered to persons referred from District (Magistrates) courts. Data on effectiveness have suggested that of 29 offender/clients who were offered an individual service between 1981 and 1987, 24 had not reoffended at 6 months follow-up. At 36 months' follow-up, 15 of these persons had not reoffended. Overall, the findings suggested that 83% of persons who accepted counseling did not reoffend during their period of deferment; 62% of their group did not reoffend during the subsequent 24 months (Collins & Tate, 1988). No control group was included, however.

Reviews of United Kingdom Agencies

A review of United Kingdom alcohol education initiatives reported questionnaire data from 20 agencies (Baldwin & Heather, 1987). Eighty percent of AECs were provided by probation/social work services, and most AECs were offered to young offenders under 30 years of age. Very low rates of referrals for female offenders were recorded by all agencies (between 1% and 5%). Ninety percent of agencies offered AECs via probation orders, while some also accepted offender/clients via a deferred sentence. The average AEC length was 12 hours, distributed over 6 sessions.

The main aim of 10 agencies (50%) was to provide "education": 6 other agencies (30%) stated the main aim was behavior change by offender/clients. Examination of AEC contents indicated that all AECs included group discussions, 95% included drink diaries, and 90% included health education materials. Since the first course in 1981, at least 240 separate AECs had been completed, with more than 1,750 "graduates" of these courses.

Seventeen agencies (85%) were committed to minimal follow-up of clients and examined drinking and/or offending behavior. None of the agencies, however, was involved in controlled evaluations, although several expressed an interest in service-based AEC evaluations.

1988 Review

An update of this review has extended the original study and confirmed many of its findings (Gamba et al., 1989). This review was based on information collected from 55 United Kingdom agencies. These data indicated that 80% of AECs continued to be provided by probation/social work services and that most services were provided for offenders younger than 30 years. Very low rates of referrals for female offenders were recorded, although three agencies ran separate AECs for females. Forty two (76%) agencies offered AECs via a probation order and 14 also accepted clients via a deferred sentence. The average AEC length was nine hours, distributed over six sessions.

The main aim of most agencies (51%) was to provide "education": 15 (27%) other agencies stated the main aim was reduced offending behavior, 11 (20%) to "increase awareness." Examination of AEC contents suggested that all AECs included group discussions and drink diaries and that 95% included health education materials. Since 1981, at least 470 separate AECs have been completed, with more than 3,400 "graduates."

Forty-seven (85%) agencies were committed to minimal follow-up of clients and examined drinking and/or offending behaviors. Four agencies were involved in a controlled evaluation (the Scottish Alcohol/Offending Evaluation Project); one other agency collected comprehensive follow-up data but did not collect pretest data, or use an experimental design with control group.

National Trends in Alcohol Education Course Development

Comparison between the two reviews of United Kingdom agencies that offered AEC services suggests specific trends in service development. In particular:

1. the statutory sector (i.e., probation/social work departments) has retained 80% involvement in national service provision
2. AECs have been directed at younger offender/clients, mostly aged 17 to 29 years
3. AECs have not generally been made available for female offender/clients
4. a trend has occurred toward more use of deferred sentencing by courts
5. a trend toward shorter AECs has occurred (reduction by 25% of average AEC length)
6. the differential emphasis (5:3) has continued on "education" (i.e., information about alcohol), rather than "behavior change" (i.e., by skills acquisition)
7. the mean number of offender/clients who have completed each AEC has been similar in both studies (i.e., 7.29 offenders per AEC in 1986; 7.23 offenders per AEC in 1988)
8. the percentage of agencies expressing a commitment to evaluation has remained constant (85%)
9. the number using controlled evaluations to investigate AEC effectiveness also has remained constant (0%).

Alcohol Education Course Components

The Dundee project was based on the original AEC model developed during a previous attempt to establish court-based service provision (Robertson & Heather, 1982a). The original model was, however, modified to account for more recent developments in social work practice and social psychology (McGuire & Priestley, 1985; Stumphauzer, 1986). In particular, the AEC was adapted to include specific skills-teaching components on "not offending" (i.e., strategies for "going straight") as well as a focus on skills in abstinence/controlled drinking. In this way, the aims of the project were derived empirically from previous work and from the pilot study.

Alcohol Education Course Contents

The AEC was designed to run for six weekly sessions, each lasting 120 minutes. The course was based on verbal presentation of materials by a course tutor, with use of audiovisual aids. Such "manualization" of intervention methods has been identified as one method to reduce uncontrolled variation in implementation (Kazdin, 1986; Shapiro & Shapiro, 1983; Stiles, Shapiro, & Elliot, 1986). Sessions involved minimal use of didactic methods, with a focus on self-help and self-learning by participants. Group discussions were used to assist peer learning where appropriate. Sessions included:

SESSION ONE: INTRODUCTION

—relationship of AEC to courts
—contracting for attendance (Stuart, 1971)
—self-recording of drinking behavior (Robertson & Heather, 1985)
—"Sensible Drinking" video (SCA, 1985b)
—drinking analysis questionnaire (Robertson & Heather, 1985)
—drink diaries (SHEG, 1985a)
—task assignment

SESSION TWO: ALCOHOL AND SELF-MONITORING

—review contract
—drink diaries
—concept of "units of alcohol"
—"That's the Limit" booklet (HEC, 1985)
—alcohol and physical health-acetate pack
—dangerous/risky/safer drinking levels
—"The Enjoyable Limit" video (SCA, 1985a)
—setting personal limits for drinking
—task assignments

SESSION THREE: DRINKING AND OFFENDING

—review progress
—drink diaries
—"tolerance" discussion
—drinking/driving discussion
—"Saturday Night and Sunday Morning" video (SHEG, 1985b)
—"Stand on Your Own Two Feet" video (SHEG, 1985c)
—personal drinking rules
—exploring personal offending behavior (McGuire & Priestley, 1985)
—task assignment

SESSION FOUR: PERSONAL VALUES AND OFFENDING—I

—review progress
—drink diaries
—offense severity exercise (McGuire & Priestley, 1985)
—reasons for and against crime (two exercises)
—choosing appropriate role models exercise
—task assignment

SESSION FIVE: PERSONAL VALUES AND OFFENDING—II

—review progress
—drink diaries
—reasons for offending and not offending exercise
—"The Victim Experience" trigger video (Baldwin, Wilson, Lancaster, & Allsop 1988)
—assertion skills exercise (McGuire & Priestley, 1985)
—effects of heavy/moderate drinking styles
—task assignment

SESSION SIX: PREVENTING REOFFENDING

—review progress
—drink diaries
—drinking analysis questionnaire
—drink diaries
—drinking analysis questionnaire
—decision-making exercise (McGuire & Priestley, 1985)
—self-monitoring skills exercise (Stumphauzer, 1986)
—self-control skills exercise (Stumphauzer, 1986)
—review AEC
—relationship of AEC to courts
—contract follow-up appointment

The revised AEC has been published as a training pack for alcohol educators (Baldwin et al., 1988).

Alcohol Education Course Rationale

The rationale for the revised AEC contents was based on several factors, which included:

1. evidence for the effectiveness of action-based strategies for this specific client group (e.g., Prochaska & Di Clemente, 1982)
2. the need to produce client-specific materials for problem behaviors (i.e., overdrinking and offending) (Blackburn, 1980)
3. the provision of direct assistance via skills teaching for problem behaviors (McGuire & Priestley, 1985)
4. the modification of behavior via skills teaching, in addition to information provision (Heather & Robertson, 1983a; Robertson & Heather, 1982a)
5. a focus on the direct modification of specific behaviors (e.g., via contingency management and self-monitoring procedures) rather than on general concepts (e.g., "alcoholic" [sic]) (Stumphauzer, 1986)
6. inclusion of principles derived from previous research in behavior therapy and behavioral self control training (Miller, 1978; Miller, Pechacek & Hamburg, 1981; Stumphauzer, 1980, 1983)
7. use of behavioral contracting to promote compliance, including: (a) details of privileges to follow responsible behaviors, (b) details of responsibilities to secure privileges, (c) system of sanctions for failure to meet responsibilities, and (d) bonus changes for compliance behaviors (Stuart, 1971)

The rationale also was based on more general assumptions about the efficacy of brief behavioral interventions with client populations (e.g., Glasgow & Rosen, 1978; Heather & Robertson, 1983a) and other beliefs about the efficacy of group-based interventions with young adult offenders (Robertson & Heather, 1982a).

Implementation of the Alcohol Education Course Package

The controlled evaluation research project in Dundee was the first attempt to measure AEC effectiveness in field settings. The ideal experimental design would have incorporated random allocation to no-intervention (or waiting list) "control" group. A complex field setting, however, involving (a) courts, (b) social workers, and (c) nonstatutory services, prevented the use of this strategy. Instead, a quasi-experimental design (Cook & Campbell, 1976, 1979) was used for one study of the evaluation research project.

Implementation of the AEC package required coordination between staff/workers in several (unconnected) agencies. Successful implementation of the AEC package thus was contingent on the cooperation and integration of workers in discrete service systems with no previous linkages. Therefore, while AEC implementation was based on a "design template" to meet evaluation research criteria, the views, needs, and preferences of local "stakeholders" also were obtained. This approach, consistent with principles of "action research" (Patton, 1982, 1983), was a deliberate strategy to involve the full range of local personnel who would be involved in subsequent AEC service provision. The eventual evaluation design thus was modified by this process of local consultation with stakeholders. This implementation also was consistent with the local development of alcohol services between statutory and nonstatutory agencies (Tether & Robinson, 1986).

The service delivery was designed to measure AEC effectiveness in several field settings. The design, establishment, maintenance, and evaluation of these services is described below as a series of related experimental interventions: Dundee (five); Glasgow (six); Perth/Forfar (seven); Noranside (eight).

Summary

The original Scottish AEC from 1981 was used to form the basis of a revised intervention program during 1985. This revised AEC, based on behavioral skills teaching with young adult offenders formed the template for the rest of the Alcohol/Offending Evaluation Project.

5

Dundee

The main study involved a comparison of behavioral AECs and talk-based AECs. This was to measure the relative impact of skills components compared to the changes that occurred from time effects and from exposure to "therapeutic" conditions of counseling.

The optimum strategy would have been to establish a set of experiments in a single field location, to test rival hypotheses about AEC effectiveness. Local constraints, however, prevented this strategy, because of implementation barriers within the court services. Specifically, it was unacceptable to the court judicial systems to start a nonintervention (control) group of offender/clients who did not receive a service. Moreover, a waiting list control also was an unacceptable strategy for the Dundee Courts.

Such problems of randomization or establishment of a waiting list control recur in applied clinical research (Kazdin, 1978). Implementation problems in field settings are commonplace (Tharp & Wetzel, 1969) and often require negotiation for a balance between an ideal research design and a pragmatic solution to fit local conditions.

A quasi-experimental design (Cook & Campbell, 1976) was used to establish the research project in other locations. This approach to fieldwork research has been established elsewhere in educational settings (e.g., Lucker, Rosenfield, Sikes, & Aronson, 1976).

In Dundee, a dual system of courts provided the structure for the criminal justice system: in practice, "less serious" offenses would be tried in the District Courts (equivalent to the Magistrates' Courts).

Experimental Hypothesis

The main hypothesis was that the effect of a behavioral AEC on drinking/offending behaviors would exceed the impact of a talk-based AEC.

Method

The preferred research design for the Dundee study was based on a no-intervention control group, which would not receive an AEC. This design was unacceptable to the local magistrates, however. (A quasi-experimental design was adopted in another study, which involved establishment of a nonequivalent group in another location).

In Dundee an alternative design was used, based on a comparison of two different types of AEC. Specifically, an attempt was made to measure the relative effectiveness of a behavioral AEC compared with a talk-based (counseling) AEC. The rationale of this comparison was to examine the effectiveness of exposure to a behavioral skills package in contrast with exposure to a dilute intervention (nondirective counseling) with minimal therapeutic content. Inclusion of a talk-based counseling AEC was based on an observation about its relative popularity as a form of service delivery in United Kingdom services for young offenders.

Owing to a slow base rate of referrals of offender/clients from the District and Sheriff Courts, it was not possible to form two separate groups using random allocation of clients. Although preferable for a robust experimental design, this procedure would have produced two problems: (a) an unacceptable delay between referral and completion of an AEC, extending beyond the six-month limit of the deferred sentence, and (b) an increased probability of attrition (dropout) from AECs by clients. For these reasons, an alternative design was used based on random assignment of conditions (behavioral AEC, talk-based AEC, behavioral AEC, etc.).

Independent Variable

The independent variable was the type of AEC: behavioral or talk-based.

Dependent Variables

The experimental design included two main dependent variables: (a) drinking behavior, and (b) offending behavior.

Subjects

A system was established for the District and Sheriff Courts to refer young offenders for Motivational Screening Interviews for suitability for an AEC. Specific criteria were established for both courts. Referrals were encouraged for offender/clients who:

1. were aged between 17 and 29 years
2. stated they would attend for an AEC interview
3. had committed two or more offenses
4. had more than half of their total offenses alcohol-related (i.e., intoxicated while offending, public order drunkenness offenses).

Referrals were encouraged for men and women, regardless of offense severity or chronicity of problems. Court officials were given repeated requests not to preselect clients according to implicit criteria outside of the experimental design.

Materials

The MSI was designed to filter offender/clients in or out of AECs, according to outcome of the interview. It was based on previous research with motivational interviewing techniques (Miller, 1983a) and adopted a similar structure to the Comprehensive Drinker Profile (Marlatt & Miller, 1984). In particular, the MSI was given to offender/clients to collect baseline data on drinking behavior, offending behavior, and "motivational information" about potential for change. In sum, the "process" of the MSI was designed to bring to the attention of the offender/client relevant information that might help to promote change attempts.

The content of behavioral AECs has been described elsewhere (see chapter 4). The content of talk-based AECs was based on nondirective counseling techniques (Hathaway, 1948; Rogers, 1957, 1975). Such counseling/discussion groups have been included as an "attention-placebo group" in comparative outcome research to exert control over nonspecific effects (Shapiro & Shapiro, 1983).

The structure of talk-based AECs was based on the use of nondirective counseling by the tutor to facilitate client learning. A restricted range of counseling skills was used extensively in AEC sessions; these were based on specific interventions. These facilitative interventions were:

1. Supportive: the tutor expresses approval, confirmation, and validation to affirm the value of the client
2. Catalytic: the tutor encourages self-directive problem-solving to promote self-direction and self-discovery by the client
3. Cathartic: the tutor encourages release of tensions (e.g., laughter, anger, fear) in the client.

The use of facilitative interventions required the tutor to be less obtrusive and more discreet, with the emphasis on the client (Heron, 1975).

With regard to treatment representativeness, the talk-based AEC was considered a relatively faithful reproduction of its counterpart in the nonresearch setting. Differences in type of counselor statement were regarded as variations in intervention-specific ingredients not expected to be held constant (Kazdin, 1986).

Background

As major "stakeholders" (Patton, 1982, 1983) in the evaluation research, extensive consultations were held with representatives of the Courts. Specifically, the proposal was presented at a monthly business meeting of the justices for their comments and suggestions. In addition, discussions with the local sheriffs produced more information about the practicalities of operating a deferred sentence project for offender/clients. Where possible, verbal statements of intent to use such a scheme were obtained from the sheriffs (n = 2) and the justices (n = 30). Furthermore, plans were made to provide written confirmation of the AEC project to individual court officials about the progress of the research. Attempts were made to solicit possible objections to the AEC research and to anticipate obstacles to progress. In particular, prolonged discussions occurred about the nature of the deferred sentence component of AECs and the public perception of this sentencing option.

In addition to discussions with court officials, several meetings were arranged with the Clerk of the Courts (the intermediary advisor between court officials and the general public) who was invited to comment on the project design. The Clerk of Courts was identified as the person most likely to influence sentencing behavior in the District Courts: in practice, the clerk would advise justices about relevant sentencing options.

Referrals

The referral of an offender/client for an MSI required an initial period of deferment (3 weeks) to allow completion of the court report. Referred offender/clients who had agreed to an MSI were informed by the court that they would receive subsequent notification of an interview: the court made a telephone call to record preliminary details, followed by written confirmation. MSI appointments were offered within 7 days of receipt of a referral: offender/clients usually were given early afternoon appointments to visit the local (nonstatutory) Council on Alcohol.

Motivational Screening Interviews

Completion of the MSI was complemented by a description to the client of the rationale for an AEC. This contained the following statement:

> You have been referred for an interview because somebody in the court believed there might be a link between your drinking and offending behavior. We have discussed this, and it seems to me there is (not) a relationship between your drinking alcohol, and getting into trouble with the police. Some/most/every time(s) you have been arrested, you have been drinking; is that correct?
>
> The reason you have been asked to visit this agency is to offer you an opportunity to join an Alcohol Education Course. You may have heard about these courses; maybe some of your drinking friends have been on one. If you decide to join an Alcohol Education Course, it works like this. I would write a recommendation to the court that you attend for a course, but you still have to argue your case when you appear in court. If the court agrees, your sentence would be deferred for 6 months to allow you to attend. Then you would return to court, and your case would be reviewed.
>
> I should tell you that I am not able to influence the decisions made by the courts: it is up to you to do this yourself. Generally, however, the courts have acted favorably to other people like you who have completed other courses. But I can't make any promises: I can't do deals with you and the courts.
>
> There is no pressure for you to attend an Alcohol Education Course. In fact, the opposite: if you feel that you have been sent under obligation, I suggest you do not attend. I am only really interested in working with people who want to do something about their drinking and getting into trouble. I think if you feel under pressure to attend, the course is not for you. You should attend only if you are really wanting to sort out your problems.
>
> What do you think? Do you think the course might be helpful to you?

The function of this monologue was to clarify to the offender/client that responsibility for change was their own decision: a set of paradoxical statements (McMullin, 1986) was used to convey to the client that *they* should decide the outcome of this meeting. Specifically, it was suggested to the client that they should not attend unless they were interested in behavioral reforms. This was designed to minimize manipulations of the client and to encourage self-direction and active participation (Mahoney, 1979).

Clients who expressed doubts about the value of an AEC were encouraged to express these feelings. Paradox was used to challenge clients' restrictive beliefs: "perhaps you feel as if you don't really have a drink problem?" or "maybe you believe it is OK to get drunk and get arrested?". Clients who affirmed these beliefs generally did not consent to an AEC and did not shift their views, despite encouragement. Clients who discontinued these beliefs were encouraged to develop their own reasons for wanting to reduce (or stop) their drinking/offending behaviors. This technique encouraged clients to "talk themselves" into an AEC. In summary, no direct attempts were made to persuade clients of a need to change their behavior, although some indirect methods were used.

If the client declined an AEC, the subsequent court procedures were explained and the person was invited to revisit the agency to read the report, before their court appearance. The report would state that the client, having visited the agency, had declined the AEC: no attempt was made to influence court sentencing.

If the client accepted an AEC, subsequent procedures were explained and the person was invited to revisit the agency to read their court report. The client was advised that they might be asked to explain their reasons for wanting to join an AEC and that this question might be put to them at their next court appearance. The relationship of the AEC to the court was explained: offenders were encouraged to acknowledge their own responsibility for behavioral reform. (For example, offenders were told directly that they might return to court having completed an AEC and then be given a prison sentence. Although this was unlikely, it helped to convey the message to the offender of taking personal responsibility.)

Written reports were sent for the subsequent appearance of the offender/client. Court reports provided basic information about drinking history, offending history, and suitability for an AEC; no additional information was disclosed. If the client had declined an AEC or if the referral was inappropriate, no other referral recommendations were made to the court. Written confirmation of outcome was sent from the courts, with dates of subsequent court appearances, if appropriate.

Pilot Study

A pilot study was started in August, 1985 to examine several aspects of the AEC service, including (a) efficiency of the referral system to/from courts, (b) the reliability and validity of the MSI, (c) AEC contents, and (d) methods of AEC presentation.

Referral System Efficiency

Referral procedures for the screening interview were influenced by constraints of the criminal justice system, which dictated that court reports should be completed within 3 weeks. The pilot study tried several strategies to set up interviews with referred clients, including telephone contact, written appointment letter, and appointment letters sent via registered mail.

Comparison of different procedures adopted during the pilot study suggested that telephone contact generally was inappropriate; although fast and direct, many clients were not on the telephone and could not be contacted. Use of registered letters had some advantages; it provided irrefutable proof of delivery. Nonetheless, some clients were already sensitized to this form of contact from court correspondence and would not sign for "formal" letters. The optimum procedure seemed to be written confirmation of an appointment with an option if desired to negotiate by telephone for a more convenient appointment.

Reliability and Validity of the Motivational Screening Interview

The MSI was based on previous work on motivational interviewing techniques (Miller, 1983; Marlatt & Miller, 1984). In particular, the Comprehensive Drinker Profile (CDP) was used to provide a framework for a pilot version of a screening instrument. The CDP was, however, overinclusive for the needs of a short screening instrument that could be administered to offender/clients in less than 60 minutes.

Several revisions of the initial pilot version produced a screening instrument that could be used to assist offender/clients make rational, data-based decisions to join/not join an AEC. Specific additions included a section on offending behavior/offending history for this client population.

Independent measures of reliability and validity were not attempted. The MSI, however, was revised using specific, detailed feedback from several interviewers who had used the instrument on many occasions. The feedback from interviewers was subjective information about ease of administration, relevance to clients' needs/problems, and conciseness of interview questions. The MSI was designed to be administered in a range of locations by different staff, without prolonged training. All potential interviewers, however, were required to observe one screening interview and to be observed during two interviews as a semiformal monitoring procedure. In addition, interviewers were given videotape feedback on interview performance.

Alcohol Education Course Contents

The pilot course was based on the original AEC model (Robertson & Heather, 1982a). The pilot course was completed by four offender/clients in November, 1985 from an initial group of 5 referrals from the District and Sheriff Courts. These participants were invited to make comments about improvements for subsequent courses.

When the pilot study was completed by all clients their comments were critical of much of the course contents. Specifically, participants did *not* value a didactic approach (e.g., provision of information sheets) and stated a preference for interactive materials (e.g., films/group discussions). In addition, most clients indicated that existing AEC contents, although helpful in the acquisition of alcohol information, did not provide information about modifying their offense behaviors. In particular, clients expressed a preference for provision of direct, practical skills to help them cope with problem situations (e.g., apprehension by police in absence of prior offense behaviors). Many clients requested skills-teaching to increase their behavioral repertoire in "nonoffending."

Many clients also stated that much of the alcohol information from the existing course was irrelevant (e.g., "facts about alcohol dependence") or overcomplicated (e.g., blood alcohol level [BAL]). Thus, whereas clients were able to understand and use the concept of "units of alcohol," several did not have the mathematical skills to use BAC/BAL tables.

Alcohol Education Course Presentation

Most clients stated a preference for a nondidactic, interactive style. Materials were presented as a source from which clients might acquire information and/or skills. Explicit attempts at teaching were rare; rather, an attempt was made to set the conditions for learning. Specifically, the AEC tutor initially encouraged clients to feel that all contributions were equally valid, without attempts at censorship of material. An atmosphere of trust was developed, with clear guidelines about confidentiality (i.e., disclosed material remained within the group) and membership (the AEC was a closed group, which did not accept new members).

Whereas the AEC contents were clearly defined, the mode of presentation was open to interpretation; the personal style of AEC tutors required standardization. (Without this standardization, the AEC would be subject to "drift," which would impede evaluation attempts.) This standardization of presentation between AEC tutors was difficult to achieve: without a prescribed style of delivery, tutors would adopt idiosyncratic methods.

Despite these potential limitations, however, presentation style was specified where possible. Much of this standardization was based on proscriptions of some styles (e.g., other-directed humor and negative feedback statements were discouraged). AEC tutors were encouraged not to be authoritative or directive (Heron, 1975).

Evaluation

The pilot study did not include a formal evaluation, although several informal monitoring methods were used. Information was requested from several sources to help ensure a wide representation of opinions. Offender/clients were asked to specify changes to AEC contents and/or presentation. The service users (i.e., court clerks) were asked to suggest modifications to enhance administrative efficiency.

In addition, information was obtained from other "stakeholders" about their view of the pilot study.

This deliberate strategy of consultation was designed to promote "ownership" of the AEC by administrative and legal management systems. It was an explicit attempt to increase perceived involvements and decrease subsequent "sabotage" attempts; this was consistent with previous attempts at behavior change in institutionalized service systems (e.g., Repucci, 1977; Repucci & Saunders, 1974).

Main Study

Support Systems for Alcohol Education Courses

The AEC service was established in a local Council on Alcohol, consistent with recent national policy initiatives (Tether & Robinson, 1985). The service could have been located in any of several settings but it was based at the nonstatutory alcohol agency to meet specific criteria. These included: (a) a nonstigmatizing service setting with a positive image, (b) an agency with knowledge about alcohol/offending problems, (c) a potential reservoir of staff/workers to acquire skills in providing AEC services and (d) a nonmedical, nonlegal environment to promote learning by offender/clients.

Initial discussions with the Council on Alcohol Director produced an agreement about the provision of AECs in the agency. In particular, all direct client services (screening interviews, AEC sessions) were based at the agency; a commitment was obtained to teach interviewing/AEC session skills to volunteer counselors. The commitment was contracted for 12 months, with options to renew as required. Training tutors at the agency also were involved to promote these new learning opportunities for counselors.

Counselors with an interest in alcohol education/offending behavior were encouraged to participate in AEC service provision and were given opportunities to observe screening interviews with clients. Counselors who expressed an interest as potential interviewers subsequently were offered opportunities to learn these skills from live interviewing, with supervized observation. Counselors were observed for a minimum of two interviews, with direct performance feedback. Although no specific measures of reliability were taken, all interviewers were observed to achieve criterion performance.

Achievement of criterion performance required successful completion of an AEC interview, with a data-based decision (and consensus with the client) on recommendation/nonrecommendation for an AEC. Counselors who achieved criterion performance also were encouraged to acquire the skills for writing court reports. Court reports written by voluntary counselors always were countersigned by a professionally qualified worker (e.g., clinical psychologist).

Some counselors who acquired skills as interviewers subsequently expressed an interest in provision of AECs. Similar in-service training methods were used as for interviewing: counselors were encouraged to attend an AEC as nonparticipant observers. Some counselors who expressed an interest in working with young offenders were then encouraged to join another AEC and copresent some sessions as a cotutor with an already trained tutor. Subsequently, these training tutors were required to present the whole AEC, with further observation by a trained tutor. Selected AEC sessions were monitored to observe preservation of "integrity" of the intervention. This three-stage model of training formed the template for subsequent service development. The provision of training of staff to administer interventions has been suggested as one method to reduce "drift" in clinical research (Kazdin, 1978).

The provision of AECs by the local Council on Alcohol thus was based on a multilevel model of implementation: (a) direct services (screening interviews/ AECs) for clients, (b) in-service teaching/training for voluntary counselors, (c) system developments (e.g., court liaison) to promote maintenance of services. This approach was consistent with a systems view of service development (e.g., Bender 1976; Praill & Baldwin, 1988).

Behavioral/Talk-Based Alcohol Education Courses

The contents and implementation of behavioral AECs have been described elsewhere (see chapter 4). (Baldwin, Heather, Lawson, Mooney, Braggins, & Robertson, 1991) Implementation of talk-based AECs required the use of specific counseling styles; in particular, supportive, catalytic, and cathartic interventions. Individual counselors implemented either behavioral or talk-based AECs (but not both) and were thus nested within interventions (Kazdin, 1986).

In addition to prescribed use of specific intervention styles, other styles were proscribed during talk-based AECs. Counselors were instructed explicitly *not* to use authoritative styles (e.g., prescriptive, informative, confrontive interventions). The rationale of nondirective AECs required counselors to adopt a consistently facilitative style. This rationale was explained to clients during the first AEC session. An AEC counselor was required to introduce themselves and ask clients to introduce themselves to the group. The tutor explained the relationship between the course and the courts and the consequences of failure to attend (or complete) AEC sessions. No formal behavioral contracts were made with clients, however.

Counselors were required to start the first session with a "rationale" for the talk-based AEC. This was based on the following statement:

> This alcohol education course is designed for you to help yourselves with your drinking and offending problems. During the sessions, however, the counselors will not be telling you what to do or giving you information or advice. They will not be giving you leaflets or showing you films; it is up to you to take the responsibility for your own learning. Although the counselors are here to help you to learn, they will not be trying to teach you things. It is up to you to take responsibility for this yourself.

The training of new counselors was completed using a similar structure as for counselors who provided behavioral AECs. Potential counselors were invited to attend an initial AEC as nonparticipant observers. Some counselors then were encouraged to attend another AEC as cocounselors; some of these counselors were encouraged to provide AECs as sole counselors with supervized monitoring. This three-stage training provided a set of progressive "filters" for potential counselors.

Behavioral Measures

At initial interview, the MSI was used to obtain baseline data on drinking and offending behaviors. As relatively unambiguous and widely accepted outcomes, this helped to focus on a "criterion-referenced" evaluation (Basham, 1986). In addition, clients were requested to complete the Drinking Attitudes Questionnaire (Robertson & Heather, 1985), GHQ (Goldberg, 1983), Offenses Questionnaire (Dight, 1976), and Severity of Alcohol Dependence Questionnaire (SADQ) (Stockwell, Murphy, & Hodgson, 1983). All clients signed consent forms.

Data on drinking behavior were obtained from two self-report drinking windows: "drinking during the past 7 days" and "period of heavy drinking during previous 6 months." Data on offending behavior were obtained from self-reported offenses since "first recorded offense" to present date.

Experimental Groups Follow-Up

Offender/clients were offered a follow-up interview 6 months after completion of an AEC and, where possible, at 12 months and 18 months. Clients were contacted by telephone or letter, and paid five pounds for completion of the interview. Consistent with attempts to control for "nonspecific" effects (Shapiro & Shapiro, 1983), follow-up interviews were completed by workers "blind" to the experimental hypothesis.

Where possible, attempts were made to locate offender/clients who had "dropped out" of the research project. Specifically, clients who had completed an initial MSI but not attended an AEC were offered five pounds for a follow-up interview. Although this did not constitute a "control" group, this sample of attrition subjects was collected to produce data on reasons for noncompletion of AECs.

Other Measures

In addition to dependent variable measurement, other data sources were collected that might have reflected changes in client behaviors. The use of multiple measures of therapeutic change has been recommended as requirements for clinical research (Kazdin, 1978). Such "multimodal" assessment, using measures based on diverse technologies, may help to counter the threats to construct validity via reliance on a single assessment modality (Shapiro & Shapiro, 1983).

District/Sheriff Court Data

Information about court appearances was obtained retrospectively for each client who had been referred for an AEC interview. These data provided detailed records of court appearances before and after an AEC. These "court appearances" did not provide a direct measure of offending behaviors, but the information provided an indirect index of offending patterns.

Police Statistics

Within the constraints of the Data Protection Act (1986), the local police department provided descriptive statistics on groups of offenders. It was impossible to obtain information on individual offending patterns but summary data on groups of offenders were provided. Data on groups of offenders who had completed behavioral or talk-based AECs were obtained. The accuracy of "recorded offenses," however, was limited by relative insensitivity of "convictions" as an index of offending behavior (Hudson, 1977) and limitations of data collection (i.e., more than three "same-category offenses" were still recorded as only three offenses).

Social Work Statistics

Social work departments were asked to provide descriptive statistics of their contacts with offender/clients: where possible, qualitative and quantitative data were obtained. This measure of social work involvement provided an index of the legal status of the offender within the formal service system. Although absence of contact with the social work department was difficult to interpret, *presence* of contact usually indicated continuation of problem behaviors.

Hospital Admissions

Screening interviews with offender/clients had indicated an increased probability of general hospital admissions, because of alcohol-related problems (e.g., head injuries, stitches from broken glass, fight damage). Information was obtained from local general hospitals about brief treatments/admissions.

Collateral Interviews

Comprehensive self-report data were obtained during baseline and follow-up interviews but information was required from other sources to corroborate (or disconfirm) this clinical perspective. Such corroborative data from collateral sources may add a unique perspective to single-source self-reports by clients (Maisto, Sobell, & Sobell, 1979; Midanik, 1982; Watson, Tilleskjor, Hoodecheck, Schow, Pucel, & Jacobs, 1983).

To provide an informal measure of reliability of clients' self-reports, a brief interview was completed at follow-up with a "collateral" source. This was based on established interview methods with collateral sources (Miller, Crawford, & Taylor, 1979). The collateral was identified and nominated at the initial screening interview as the person "closest" to the client (i.e., spouse, lover, best friend, parent). Consent was obtained from the client for this interview, which was completed by direct interview or by telephone.

Results

Seventy eight offender/clients were referred for assessment for an AEC. Thirteen offender/clients completed a talk-based AEC and 15 completed a behavioral AEC. Mean age of the talk-based AEC was 19.6 years (range 17.8–21.6 years); 20.4 years (range 19.0–24.1 years) on the behavioral AEC. Between-groups comparisons of talk-based/behavioral AEC data produced no significant differences on qualitative/quantitative variables (t tests, independent samples) or on qualitative variables (chi-square test).

Follow-Up Rates

Follow-up data are reported for 9 (69%) clients in the talk-based AEC (mean follow-up time 8.6 months; range 6–12 months). In the "assessment only" group, there was a mean age of 20.2 years (range 16.3–27.8 years) and a mean follow-up time of 9 months (range 6–12 months).

Seventeen subjects who completed an initial MSI but did not complete an AEC were reinterviewed for a follow-up interview (mean follow-up time, 11 months; range 8–14 months).

Comparisons were made between subjects who completed an AEC and a follow-up interview, with subjects who completed an AEC and who dropped out of the study following AEC completion. There were no differences between the two groups, with three exceptions. The "follow-up group" were younger (mean x = 20 years) than the "dropout" group (mean x = 23 years)(p ≤ 0.005; t test); the first group had fewer children on average (0.2; 0.9)(p ≤ 0.05; t test); 18/18 of the "follow-up" group were single, compared with 7/10 of the "dropout" group (p ≤ 0.05; chi-square).

Analysis of Change at Follow-Up

Analysis of variance revealed a significantly different interaction effect of the course and time on comparisons between behavioral and talk-based AECs for average number of alcohol units per drinking session. Before/after comparisons revealed an average increase on talk-based AECs (7.7–16.6) and a decrease on behavioral AECs (10.0–6.7)(two-way ANOVA; p ≤ 0.05). (See Table 5.1.).

Between-groups comparisons of talk-based/behavioral AEC outcome data produced no significant differences on any quantitative variables (t tests, independent samples), or qualitative variables (chi-square test).

Examination of the within-group differences of the talk-based AEC at baseline and follow-up did not produce significant statistical differences (t tests, related samples).

Within-group differences of the behavioral AEC at baseline and follow-up produced a significant reduction in self-reported conviction rates from 2.1–0.7 (p ≤ 0.01) and a significant reduction in self-reported "life problems" (4.2–1.6) (p ≤ 0.05) (t tests, related samples). In addition to these differences of within-group changes at baseline and follow-up, several trends emerged that indicate

TABLE 5.1. Summary Data of Dundee AEC Study.

	Talk-based AEC		Behavioral AEC	
	Baseline	Follow-up	Baseline	Follow-up
1.	26.4	34.6 NS	32.1	22.6 NS
2.	7.7	16.6 NS	10.1	6.7 NS
3.	2.7	1.1 NS	2.1	0.9 $p \leq 0.01$
4.	6.0	4.7 NS	7.4	4.1 $p \leq 0.05$
5.	3.1	3.3 NS	4.2	1.6 NS
6.	1.0	0.3 NS	1.5	0.9 NS
7.	6.8	3.1 NS	2.1	4.4 NS
8.	6.2	0.6	1.1	0.4 NS
9.	76.0	75.0 NS	73.0	82.0 NS
10.	3.8	4.3 NS	6.0	4.1 NS
11.	6.3	7.0 NS	11.5	6.8 NS
12.	15.3	14.6 NS	19.3	16.5 NS

1. mean number of units per week; 2. average number of units per drinking session; 3. conviction rates (self-reported); 4. mean number of "life problems"(alcohol-related and nonalcohol-related); 5. mean number of "life problems"(alcohol-related only); 6. mean number offenses against property (self-reported); 7. mean number offenses against rules/regulations (self-reported); 8. mean number offenses against persons (self-reported); 9. confidence ratings ([p] stick to drinking level); 10. mean values MAST; 11. mean values Attitudes to Drinking Questionnaire; 12. mean values General Health Questionnaire. NS = Not Significant

statistically nonsignificant but clinically relevant modifications in drinking/offending behaviors.

Examination of qualitative data from between-group comparisons at baseline and follow-up did not produce statistically significant differences, with the exception of level of alcohol consumption; clients from the behavioral course showed a significant reduction in their level of drinking ($p \leq .01$, Wilcoxon signed-ranks, matched pairs test). On average, clients were changing from level 4 (steady drinker with binges) to level 3 (steady drinker).

Subject Attrition

Where possible, interviews were completed with clients who had completed an MSI assessment interview, but had not completed an AEC. Data from such clients were pooled to form an "assessment only" group. These clients completed identical follow-up procedures as other clients.

Analysis of variance techniques indicated several significantly different interactions of intervention and time between behavioral AEC, talk-based AEC and "assessment only" groups on average number of units per drinking session. Before/after comparisons revealed changes in all groups: behavioral AEC (10.0–7.0); talk-based AEC (8.0–17.0); "assessment only" (15.0–10.0)(two-way ANOVA $p \leq 0.05$). Further comparisons between these groups revealed significant differences between some pairs (talk-based AEC/behavioral AECs; $p \leq .05$)(talk-based AECs/"assessment only"; $p \leq .05$).

Preintervention

Between-groups comparisons of talk-based AECs, behavioral AECs, and "assessment only" groups produced no significant differences on any quantitative variables (one-way ANOVA; independent samples) or on qualitative variables (chi-square test).

Follow-up comparisons between the three groups did not produce significant differences on quantitative variables (one-way ANOVA; independent samples) or on qualitative variables (chi-square test).

Examination of before/after within-group differences indicated several significant differences in the "assessment only" group; a reduction in conviction rate from 3.6 to 1.2 per year ($p \leq .05$; t test, related samples); a shift in type of drinking pattern from level 4 to level 3, that is, from steady drinkers with binges to steady drinkers without binges ($p \leq .05$; Wilcoxon signed-ranks matched pairs test).

District/Sheriff Court Data

Data on recorded offenses were obtained from District and Sheriff Courts in Dundee, via examination of court records. Offending rates in the 12 months after completion of talk-based or behavioral AECs were compared between groups, although no significant differences were observed.

Analysis of variance techniques revealed no significantly different interactions on intervention and time (two-way ANOVA).

Within the behavioral AEC group, however, clients' offending rates reduced from 3.11 in the 12 months prior to an AEC to .66 in the 12 months after an AEC (t tests, related samples) ($p \leq .005$).

Within the talk-based AEC group, clients' offending rates reduced from 3.66 in the 12 months prior to an AEC to 0.81 in the 12 months after an AEC (t tests, related samples) ($p \leq .05$).

Within the "assessment only" group, clients' offending rates reduced significantly from 1.83 in the 12 months prior to an assessment interview to 0.71 in the subsequent 12 months ($p \leq .01$) (t tests, related samples).

Data also were collected among a fourth group of clients who had been referred for an assessment interview but who had not attended. This "no assessment/no interview" group produced no significant differences in within-group comparisons.

Police Statistics

Data from criminal statistics at the police department were used to make some comparisons between groups of clients. While limitations of the Data Protection Act (1986) prevented release of data on the offending behavior of individual clients, data on three groups were obtained: talk-based AEC group, behavioral AEC group, and "assessment only" (attrition) group.

Offending rates were calculated for 15 months follow-up (15 months after initial MSI for "assessment only" group) and adjusted to provide an annual estimate.

Analysis of variance techniques did not indicate any significantly different interaction effects between the four groups: (behavioral AEC, talk-based AEC, "assessment only," "no assessment/no interview" two-way ANOVA).

Preintervention between-groups comparisons did not indicate any significant differences (one-way ANOVA). Follow-up between-groups comparisons produced significant differences. Several significant differences in average number of recorded offenses per year between specific pairs were found:

—talk-based AECs (.67 per year) and no assessment/no AEC group (3.58 per year) ($p \le .001$)
—talk-based AECs (.67 per year and "assessment only" group (2.94 per year) ($p \le .005$)
—behavioral AEC (1.31 per year) and "no assessment/no AEC" group (3.58 per year) ($p \le .05$)
—behavioral AEC (1.31 per year) and "assessment only" group (2.94 per year) ($p \le .05$)(one-way ANOVA)

Within-groups comparisons produced several significant changes in average number of recorded offenses per year pre-intervention and follow-up.

A before/after reduction was observed in the behavioral AEC group (3.00 per year to 1.31 per year) ($p \le .05$); in the talk-based AEC group (2.93 per year to .67 per year) ($p \le .001$); in the "assessment only" group 4.00 per year to 2.94 per year ($p \le .05$) (t tests, related samples).

Social Work Data

Data on "client contacts" were provided by the social work department. These data did not provide qualitative information about the nature of the contact, and only recorded quantitative information as the "occurrence of at least one contact" by the client with the social work department.

"Occurrence of contact" was calculated for the 15 months follow-up (15 months after intitial MSI for "assessment only" group).

"Contact with social work department" varied between groups:

—talk-based AEC 4/15 (27%)
—behavioral AEC 7/13 (54%)
—"assessment only" 15/27 (56%)

Hospital Admissions

Data were obtained for brief treatments (or admissions) to local general hospitals for talk-based and behavioral AEC groups. An idiosyncracy of local health service policy on admissions data prevented collection of information about "assessment only" group.

Two offenders from talk-based AECs were admitted to local general hospitals in the 15 months following completion of an AEC; one client was admitted after a suicide attempt and the other after a head injury from a fight. Both occurred following alcohol intoxication.

Two offenders from behavioral AECs were admitted to local general hospitals in the 15 months after completion of an AEC; one client was admitted following a drug overdose and the other after a fight. Neither admission was alcohol-related.

Collateral Interviews

A range of collateral sources was used, including spouse, girlfriend, same-sex friend, opposite-sex friend, father, mother, brother, sister, "other" (e.g., social workers). Collateral interviewees were asked a range of questions about the progress of the client. In particular, collaterals were asked to rate improvements/deterioration in the specific domains of drinking and offending behaviors.

Five-point rating scales were used to obtain agreement/disagreement with clients about improvement or deterioration of drinking and offending. In general, where discrepancies occurred, collaterals tended to overestimate clients' drinking behavior. Mostly, however, collaterals' estimates of client improvement/deterioration of drinking and offending behaviors agreed with those of the client.

Ratings of improvement/deterioration on "drinking behavior" produced different levels of agreement between the groups:

—talk-based   88%
—behavioral   71%
—"assessment only"   88%

Ratings of improvement/deterioration on "getting into trouble with the law" produced identical levels of agreement between groups:

—talk-based   100%
—behavioral   100%
—"assessment only"   100%

Comparisons between results obtained from talk-based/behavioral groups did not produce significant differences; comparisons of both groups with the "assessment only" group did not produce significant differences (chi-square test).

Discussion

The potency of the results should be viewed in the context of the few clients who completed an AEC and who were interviewed successfully at follow-up. Despite the inherent limitations of "small n" studies (e.g., Cohen, 1962), however, some trends may be derived with caution from the data. The lack of obtained differences on between-groups preintervention comparisons suggest that the constitution of the talk-based and behavioral AEC groups was similar and that observed differences at follow-up could be attributed to the nature of the intervention.

The initial similarity between talk-based and behavioral AEC groups suggests that subsequent observed differences were not due to differential selection effects or assignment to groups. This apparent similarity may be questionable, however, given the use of an attention placebo design. As a control for nonspecific effects, it is the least preferred strategy (Kazdin & Wilcoxon, 1976) given its limitations of rationale and its dissimilarity to behavioral methods. In addition, comparative outcome studies have limitations as a primary means to resolve questions about alternative interventions, due to the sheer number of techniques compared. Moreover, placebo control groups may not serve as a primary test of efficacy of psychosocial interventions (Parlott, 1986). Although placebo control studies may offer information about how an intervention works, they are not designed as a unique test of whether an intervention works (Basham, 1986).

The low percentage (36%) of offender/clients who completed an AEC (n = 28) following initial court referral (n = 78), however, indicates much self-selection by clients for this intervention. Offender/clients who completed an AEC may not have been representative of the whole population of referred clients. This may have created some target problems (Kazdin, 1978) and has raised the question as to whether offender/clients referred by courts for AECs are representative of the total population. In addition to selection biases from attrition, the power of the study may have diminished over the course of follow-up assessment (Kazdin, 1986).

Following initial court referral, many clients (n = 50) decided at the MSI not to attend an AEC, or subsequently dropped out of the study. Many clients, for example, declined an AEC because they did not want a deferred sentence "hanging over them" and preferred to risk a fine or custodial sentence in the court at their next appearance. Thus, while the experimental design included a randomized sequence of interventions, the research study may have been flawed by nonrepresentative sampling.

Follow-up rates of 60% and 69% indicate similar attrition rates by offender/clients in both groups. Successful completion of follow-up interviews with more than two thirds of all subjects suggests that data obtained were somewhat representative of the total cohort; it is also consistent with typical follow-up rates obtained in the forensic field (Spence, 1979). A minimum follow-up period of 8 months for all subjects suggests that obtained results may have generality across time and thus provide some evidence of maintenance of intervention effects.

Use of comparative designs reduce the probability of statistically significant findings, because of smaller effect sizes (Basham, 1986; Shapiro & Shapiro, 1983). Whereas comparative designs may be more conservative in finding statistically significant group differences, they are less vulnerable to several validity threats. Also, comparative studies may be inherently limited in their potency to resolve the central question about relative effectiveness (Kazdin, 1986; Luborsky & Singer, 1975).

Examination of within-group changes suggests both types of intervention produced some positive responses and some signs of adaptive behavior change. Specifically, reductions were observed at follow-up for talk-based and behavioral AECs for mean number of units per week, self-reported offending rates, mean number of "life problems," mean number of offenses against property, mean number of offenses against other persons, and mean values of GHQ.

Some follow-up reductions were recorded for behavioral AECs but not for talk-based AECs; specifically, average number of units per drinking session, mean number of "all life problems," mean values of MAST, and mean values of Attitudes to Drinking Questionnaire. In addition, confidence ratings of perceived ability to adhere to a specific drinking level improved after a behavioral AEC but were reduced following a talk-based AEC. One result against this general trend was recorded: mean number of self-reported offenses against rules and regulations decreased in the talk-based AEC but increased in the behavioral AEC.

Examination of drinking patterns at follow-up suggested that among clients whose pattern shifted, those in behavioral AECs were more likely to change to a less heavy drinking pattern than clients in talk-based AECs.

Results obtained from the "assessment only" group, however, suggested that some of the changes observed from AEC interventions may also be obtained from more brief interventions (i.e., assessment screening interviews). This finding is consistent with similar findings with other drinking clients (Miller, Sovereign, & Krege, 1988).

Despite the improvements obtained at follow-up for AECs, some improvements may have been due to regression effects. In particular, changes on various assessment measures on different occasions may reflect a reversion of scores toward the mean. This statistical regression effect is of particular salience with the population of offender/clients, who tend to score at the extremes on each assessment occasion.

Other threats to internal validity include the possibility of reactivity of the research context: reactive assessment may have occurred among clients who were aware of the research focus on particular behaviors. In addition, reactive experimental arrangements may have occurred from clients' awareness of their participation in a special program. Talk-based and behavioral AECs may have produced different degrees of experimental reactivity.

Also, the "nesting" of counselors within different interventions prevented separation of the impact of counselors and intervention effects. The counselors and interventions may have been confounded, and differences obtained could be reinterpreted as a difference in counselors who provided AECs. Specifically, different kinds of counselors may be attracted to different kinds of interventions. While age (25–30 years) and range of experience (2–3 years) were similar in all counselors, it would have been preferable to cross counselors with interventions.

Other threats to internal validity include the influence of extraneous effects and temporal intervention (AEC) group composition effects. In particular, without a no-intervention control group it is impossible to be certain that both types of AEC groups were not influenced by extraneous variables (e.g., variations in court disposal policy, climate of sentencing, cycles of unemployment). In addition, temporal group composition effects may have differentially influenced outcome of AEC interventions (e.g., seasonal variations in AEC operation).

Summary

Small sample size of offender/clients who completed talk-based and behavioral AECs limits generalizability of outcome measures. Despite several threats to internal and external validity imposed by limitations of the research design, however, the findings lend some support for a modest positive effect of both types of AEC. Furthermore, some additional gains are observed in offender/clients who complete a behavioral AEC. Differential client reactions to different AECs (i.e., attrition, untoward side effects, adherence to the program, attendance, and satisfaction) may favor use of behavioral AECs. Some gains may also occur in clients who complete brief assessments (screening interviews).

6

Glasgow

The main (Dundee) study was designed to evaluate the effectiveness of a behavioral AEC compared with a talk-based AEC. Implementation problems in this urban setting raised specific questions about how these difficulties might be resolved in another location.

The low base rate of referrals in the Dundee District and Sheriff Courts raised fundamental questions about whether similar problems would occur in other settings. In addition, a robust experimental design would require that effects obtained in one location could be reproduced in other, similar settings. Therefore, a replication study was planned for subsequent evaluation.

The relative degree of success in reproduction of effects obtained would provide one test of generalization of client improvement in new environments. The main aim of the replication study was to keep constant the experimental variables in a new setting and to observe subsequent similarities and differences in experimental effects.

An initial meeting was completed with stipendiary justices (paid magistrates) in the Glasgow District Court, by arrangement with the Clerk of the Court. The court officials were highly supportive of the implementation of such a scheme; many people expressed a positive intention to use the service, if established. Court officials were encouraged to suggest modifications or alterations to the AEC to promote their personal investment and subsequent "ownership" (Patton, 1982, 1983).

Experimental Hypothesis

The experimental hypothesis was identical to the hypothesis in the main study. As a replication study, the same experimental design was adopted from the main study. Identical criteria were used to recruit subjects for the replication study. The same form and content were used for AEC implementation.

Method

Procedure

All Glasgow stipendiary justices (n = 5) favored the implementation of AEC services; several officials observed that in "the busiest courts in Europe" new sentencing options would be welcomed.

At this stage, the Glasgow Sheriff Courts were not approached; the base-rate of referrals was expected to exceed the capacity of staff to provide AEC services. In addition, the District Courts were expected to produce higher referral rates than the Sheriff Courts, because of the "perceived seriousness" of offender/clients who appeared in the Sheriff Courts. (The Dundee study had indicated a tendency for custodial sentencing options to be used in the Sheriff Courts.)

A second meeting with the stipendiary magistrates confirmed their support for the AEC service. An agreement was made to provide regular written communications about progress and to attend quarterly judicial business meetings to provide feedback and information about AEC effectiveness. The written "progress bulletins" also would be sent individually to all nonstipendiary magistrates (n = 195). In addition, an outline of the structure and function of the AEC service was sent to all court officials before implementation of the service.

Referrals

The same referral criteria were used as in other experimental studies. Individual offender/clients were referred to the local nonstatutory Council on Alcohol for a screening interview. This procedure required an initial deferment of 3 weeks, during which time the person would attend for interview. On completion of the MSI, a report was sent to the District Court for the next appearance, with information about suitability for an AEC. With the exception of exclusion from Sheriff Court referrals, all procedures were identical to the main study.

As a replication study, the contents of behavioral and talk-based AECs were unmodified from the original study: attempts were made to maintain the same presentation style.

The AEC service was established in the local Council on Alcohol, consistent with the main study design. Initial discussions with the agency director produced an agreement about establishment and location of the service for 12 months. A similar commitment was made to teach interviewing skills and AEC presentation skills to volunteer counselors, according to local needs.

Counselors with an interest in young offenders/alcohol education were encouraged to acquire information and skills, using an identical training template as in the main study. A team of four counselors achieved criterion with the MSI; two counselors were trained to provide behavioral AECs and one counselor was trained to provide talk-based AECs. The same multilevel approach for establishment of AEC services was used. Attempts were made to work directly at three levels with clients, counseling staff, and support systems (e.g., training programs).

The main aim of the Glasgow project was to achieve a replication of the main study. Specifically, the study was designed to measure the relative effectiveness of a behavioral AEC compared with a talk-based counseling AEC.

Secondary aims of the replication study were to compare base-rate referrals in another setting, and investigate the degree of generalizability into a novel setting, using the same design and structure.

Behavioral Measures

A range of measures was used to measure the impact of AECs on drinking and offending behaviors of clients.

Baseline

At initial interview, the MSI was used to obtain baseline data on drinking and offending behaviors. In addition, clients completed the Drinking Attitudes Questionnaires, MAST, SADQ, and Offenses Questionnaire. Data on drinking behavior were obtained from the two self-report drinking windows: data on offending behavior were obtained from self-reported offenses since first recorded offenses to present date. All clients signed consent forms.

Follow-Up

Offender/clients were offered an interview 6 months after completion of an AEC. Clients were contacted by telephone or letter and paid five pounds for completion of the interview. Follow-ups were completed by research workers blind to the experimental hypothesis.

Collateral Interviews

To provide one measure of reliability of clients' self-reports, a brief interview was completed at follow-up with a "collateral" source. This person had been identified and nominated at the initial MSI as the person "closest" to the client. Consent was obtained from the client for this interview, which was completed by direct interview (or by telephone when not possible).

Results

A total of 64 offender/clients were referred for assessment to an AEC. Four offender/clients completed a talk-based AEC (mean age = 25 years) (range 23.9–26.0 years) and nine completed a behavioral AEC (range 17.1–28.3 years).

Between-groups comparisons of talk-based/behavioral AEC data produced no significant differences on any quantitative variables (t tests). Similarly, comparisons of differences in qualitative variables produced no significant differences between talk-based and behavioral AECs (chi-square test).

Follow-Up Rates

Follow-up data were collected for two (50%) offender/clients in the talk-based AEC group (mean follow-up time, 9 months) (range 6–12 months) and for six (66%) clients in the behavioral AEC group (mean follow-up time, 9 months) (range 6–12 months).

Comparisons were made on prevention measures between subjects who completed an AEC and a follow-up interview with subjects who then completed an AEC and who dropped out of the study. There were no differences between the two groups, with one exception. In the "follow-up" group, 0/5 clients were strong beer drinkers; in the "dropout" group 2/8 clients were strong beer drinkers (p ≤ .05; chi-square).

Analysis of Change at Follow-Up

The few clients who completed an AEC and a follow-up interview prevented the meaningful application of statistical techniques. (To address some of the problems created by "small n" samples obtained in the two studies, data from both studies subsequently were combined in a single analysis.)

Within-group differences of clients who completed a behavioral AEC suggested a decrease in the amount of alcohol-related life problems from baseline (5.0) to follow-up (1.8). Also, on average, this group moved to lower drinking levels, from level 4 (steady drinker with binges) to level 3 (steady drinker). Other clinically relevant modifications in drinking/offending behavior also were observed in clients who completed a behavioral AEC. (See Table 6.1.).

Discussion

The main limitation of this study was the failure to recruit adequate numbers of subjects to ensure representative sampling for subsequent statistical analysis. All results interpretations are limited in generalizability.

The year-end total of 64 clients represents an average of one referral per week for initial assessment interviews from the "busiest courts in Europe" (Cuthbert, 1988).

Several strategies were used during the 12 months of service provision to increase the base-rate of referrals for initial assessments. These included: (a) visits to the District Court, (b) written progress reports on individual client outcome, (c) liaison visits to the Clerk of Court, (d) circulated reports on study progress, and (e) published reports in local media. Monitoring of referral rates throughout 12 months suggested that none of these interventions exerted an adequate effect on referrals for AEC assessments.

TABLE 6.1. Summary Data of Glasgow AEC Study.

	Talk-based AEC		Behavioral AEC	
	Baseline	Follow-up	Baseline	Follow-up
1.	0.0	49.0	16	29.8
2.	0.0	27.0	4.2	10.8
3.	126.5	139.5	106.7	126.0
4.	0.9	0.0	3.6	2.5
5.	3.5	4.5	6.7	5.0
6.	1.5	2.0	5.0	1.8
7.	8.0	26.0	5.2	14.0
8.	50.0	87.5	64.0	73.3
9.	—	4.0	9.0	11.2
10.	—	5.0	2.0	2.5

1. mean number of units per week; 2. average number of units per drinking session; 3. average number of units ("heavy drinking period"); 4. mean offending rates; 5. mean number of "life problems" (alcohol-related and nonalcohol-related); 6. mean number of "alcohol-related life problems"; 7. mean value "ideal drinking levels" (units per week); 8. mean percentage confidence ratings ([p] stick to drinking levels); 9. mean number of offenses against rules (self-reported); 10. mean number of offenses against persons (self-reported).

Discussion of this topic with the Clerk of the Court and several justices from the court suggested that the actual reasons for low referral rates were related to several other factors, including: (a) prevailing court sentencing policy, (b) attitudes, beliefs, and behavior of court officials, and (c) court workload.

First, the prevailing court sentencing policy at the time of the research evaluation was a tough "law and order" climate; sentencing alternatives that did not fit with this policy generally were not favored. Second, attitudes, beliefs, and behaviors of justices often were incompatible with the "reeducational" perspective of AECs. In particular, many justices openly challenged the utility of educational options for sentencing by District Court officials. In addition, many justices maintained traditional beliefs about alcohol and alcohol-related offending (e.g., disease/illness models) with a parallel view that only total abstinence was appropriate for offender/clients with drinking problems.

Third, several court clerks and some justices made observations about the relationship of the AEC scheme to their court workloads. Specifically, a recommendation of an AEC in the court would double, triple, or quadruple the "court list" (workload): initial deferment of an offender/client would require their reappearance in court after the assessment interview to receive their sentence. Subsequent deferment to attend an AEC required the offender/client to reappear in court at least once (and possibly twice) more.

These procedures were implemented in courts that were already working beyond their capacity: nonparticipant observations in these District Courts confirmed that each court often processed more than 60 offender/clients in 150-minute sittings.

Thus, in the context of such busy court schedules, implementation of procedures that increased workload (in the short term) may have been counterproductive.

Specifically, it may have overloaded a system that was unable to support any new methods that threatened to multiply short-term demands on very limited resources, despite possible long-term benefits.

The combination of these three factors may have produced a situation in which only limited progress could be achieved in the short-term (i.e., 12 months). The delay between AEC completion and follow-up interview exacerbated this situation; meaningful feedback to the courts about client progress was not possible before the end of the 12-month contracted service provision. This created a situation in which courts were required to refer clients "in good faith," without evidence of success. Also, "system change" may require much longer timescales: estimates for such organizational modifications have ranged from 36 to 60 months (Georgiades & Phillimore, 1975).

In addition to system variables of noncompliance within the court, specific attrition problems differentially affected the talk-based AECs. Thus, whereas behavioral AECs were completed with 80% of the original starting group, confirming similar completion rates in the main study, three attempts were required to complete one talk-based AEC. Most clients dropped out of talk-based AECs after the initial session, preventing continuation of the group.

This attrition phenomenon could be attributable to other factors (e.g., AEC counselor style), but this finding corroborated similar difficulties in completion of talk-based AECs in the main (Dundee) study, where client attrition had been a recurrent problem.

One conclusion has been that offender/clients may prefer the high degree of structure offered by a behavioral AEC and do not drop out of a course designed to meet their behavioral needs.

Despite the unresolved methodological limitations of the study, some findings from the main (Dundee) study were replicated. The decrease in offending rates in the Glasgow behavioral AEC group was consistent with the findings of the original study. Increases in the average number of units drunk per week from baseline to follow-up in the behavioral AEC group (16 to 29 units) suggested that offender/clients who completed behavioral AECs had increased their overall drinking during this period. This tendency to drink to a "safer recommended limit" may be a problem for health educators. Alternatively, the difference in drinking levels may be artifactual: 16 units may reflect drinking levels prior to apprehension by police which have decreased following legal proceedings, whereas 29 units represents an accurate report of drinking levels more than 1 year "postapprehension." On balance, the impact of legal apprehension remains difficult to assess.

Examination of Table 6.1 suggests that while small cell sizes precluded rigorous statistical analysis, several trends corroborate some findings of the main study. In particular, completion of a behavioral AEC may have inoculated offender/clients from very heavy drinking periods in the future. Thus, despite the observation that on average offender/clients may drink "up to safer levels," this may nevertheless prevent or deter even heavier drinking. Neither form of AEC, however, prevented offender/clients from excessive drinking during periods of relapse: despite the general attenuating effect of the behavioral AEC on drinking levels, this was of insufficient potency to affect drinking behavior markedly when relapse periods occurred.

The trend toward reduction of "life problems" following completion of a behavioral AEC was consistent with other findings that after reductions in drinking/offending behaviors, improvements occurred in related life domains. Observed increases in number of self-reported offenses against rules/regulations and against persons following completion of a behavioral AEC were contradicted by reductions in rates of offending from preintervention to follow-up. One explanation suggests that, although offenders have been apprehended less often, they have increased offending behavior. The absence of data from the talk-based AEC group has prevented adequate comparisons: it is a variation from the main study, which suggested a general reduction in offending following completion of a behavioral AEC.

Other methodological limitations of this design have exerted restrictions on generalizability. These limitations include threats to internal validity, such as the influence of extraneous effects and temporal group composition effects. Threats to external validity include statistical regression effects, nonrepresentative sampling, reactivity of research context, and nonrepresentativeness of research context. Notwithstanding these limitations, a part-replication of the main study was achieved, in particular from process variables.

Summary

Despite methodological limitations produced by a study with very small cell sizes, some findings corroborate some outcome data from the main study. Moreover, they corroborate some of the findings of process data, which reflect the difficulties of establishing AECs as court services. A part-replication of the main study was achieved (Baldwin, Cuthbert, Greer, McCluskey, & Lawson, 1991).

7

Perth/Forfar

The main Dundee study was designed to compare the effectiveness of two different AEC interventions. A complementary study also was required to compare the impact of an AEC intervention with a no-intervention control group.

The establishment of an intervention/control group design in a single forensic setting (i.e., Dundee courts) proved unresolvable; court officials were not prepared to withhold services from clients to form a control group, due to "ethical" objections. Despite the incongruence of this position in the content of wholly unevaluated service systems, it was impossible to contract this agreement with the courts.

Protracted discussions in Perth court services, however, produced an agreement to form a no-intervention control group, with the contingency that subsequently a full AEC court service would be provided, subject to effectiveness.

Given the practical limitations of the open field, the original design was modified to include this comparison sample from a similar client population.

This revised design was based on a no-intervention control group of offender/clients identified by the Perth Sheriff Courts as potentially eligible for an AEC: these clients would be interviewed and reinterviewed to examine time effects. An equivalent group of offender/clients was identified by the Forfar Sheriff Courts and offered an AEC.

Experimental Hypothesis

The main hypothesis was that the impact of an information-based AEC on drinking/ offending behaviors would be greater than the effects measured by a no-intervention control (i.e., time effects, random effects, maturation, spontaneous remission). This was based on the rationale that an information-only AEC (with no specific skills components) would impact on drinking/offending behaviors.

Method

The Perth/Forfar study was designed to examine the impact of an AEC on a group of clients relative to the impact of time effects only on a similar group of clients. This nonequivalent control group design has been used in similar studies of the effects of educational materials on student behavior (e.g., Lucker et al., 1976). This quasi-experimental design also has been used in similar settings with other client populations (Schulz & Harman-Hanusa, 1978).

The independent variable was the information-based AEC or no intervention control.

The design included two main dependent variables: (a) drinking behavior, and (b) offending behavior.

Subjects

Subjects for the Perth and Forfar groups were recruited according to the same criteria from the main study.

Materials

With the exception of the MSI, no materials were required for the no-intervention control group from Perth.

The Forfar AEC was based on a similar design and presentation to the original AEC model. The Forfar AEC had been developed from the original model with some modifications, and was used to change the drinking/offending patterns of clients. The Forfar AEC was, therefore, a derivation of the original AEC model.

Examination of its contents suggested that it was based on 80% provision of information, 10% group discussion, and 10% skills teaching. The predominance of this type of content allowed the evaluation of an AEC based on information-provision as the method of behavior change. As an information-based AEC, the Forfar course was similar in content to the predominant model in England (Gamba et al., 1989). This study thus allowed an investigation of an information-based AEC, compared with a no-intervention control condition.

The presentation style was similar to that used in the original study, with a nondidactic nonauthoritarian approach to information-provision. An identical method of counselor training was used as in the main study; a potential counselor was invited to observe the first AEC and then to teach a second AEC.

Procedures

Initial discussions were completed with the two sheriffs and the court liaison officer (social worker). It was agreed that eligible candidates would be identified during Sheriff Court proceedings each day. Identification of candidates was the joint responsibility of the sheriff and the court liaison officer. The same referral criteria were applied as in the main study. Weekly lists of names, addresses, and dates of birth were sent from the court.

Interviews

All potential clients were contacted by letter. This initial contact letter requested the involvement of young offenders in a research study:

> Dear XYZ
> I write to see if you would be interested to take part in a research study that is looking at drinking patterns in the under-30s.
>
> Your involvement would require you to be interviewed twice by one of our staff in complete confidence. The interviewer would ask questions about your drinking and other behaviors during the previous 6 months. The first interview would take place during the next 4 weeks and the second in several months' time.
>
> The interviews can be completed in your own home or at the Social Work Department. If you agree to join the research study, I am asking you to choose where and when you prefer to be interviewed.
>
> This interview will be in complete confidence: no information will be made available to the police, courts, social workers, or anyone else. The interviews are for the research study only, and will not be given to other people.
>
> There is a small financial reward for agreeing to join the research study. We can offer you ten pounds; five pounds when you have completed your first interview. Another five pounds will be given to you when you have completed your second interview, in several months' time.

Baseline

At initial interview, the same measures were obtained as in the main study. These included MSI, Drinking Attitudes Questionnaire, MAST, SADQ, GHQ, and Offenses Questionnaire. All clients signed consent forms.

These measures were repeated at the second interview. In addition, interviewers obtained information from a collateral source (person nominated by the client) to provide additional information about the drinking of the client. Interviewers were blind to the experimental hypothesis.

Forfar Procedure

Initial discussions were completed with the sheriff in the court. With the exception of vacations, the same sheriff operated the court list throughout; thus, it was not necessary to involve the court liaison officer because this project had been initiated by the sheriff. Identification of potential candidates was the sole responsibility of the sheriff. Identical referral criteria were used as in the Dundee and Perth studies. Eligible candidates were referred to the Social Work Department at Forfar for assessment interviews.

Baseline Interviews

Offender/clients were interviewed by a senior social worker or a research assistant using the MSI to assess AEC eligibility. Similar procedures were used as in the main study. The interview was used to make decisions with the client about suitability for an AEC.

Clients who agreed to join an AEC were recommended to the court for a deferred sentence. Clients signed consent forms to acknowledge their participation.

Support Systems for AECs

It was not possible to use a nonstatutory alcohol agency to support AECs, as outreach services had not been extended to distal rural centers. Thus, the social work department was incorporated into the template of AEC services. Although it was not an ideal choice as a statutory service (due to the mandate functions of social workers), it was the only agency that could be inlvoved in AEC implementation.

The social work department offered physical facilities and some staffing supports to establish and maintain an AEC service to the Sherrif Court. Discussions with the senior social worker produced an agreement to maintain and evaluate the AEC service. This commitment was contracted for 12 months, with subsequent review. A second social worker was encouraged to acquire the prerequisite skills to complete initial interviews and provide AECs.

The AEC service was established according to the principles of the main study, with similar rationale, planning and implementation. Some operational differences existed, however, because of the involvement of a statutory (social work) and not a nonstatutory (alcohol agency) service. Specifically, self-disclosure by offender/clients within AEC sessions may have been attenuated by the mandate role of social workers to report (and act on) information about offending behaviors; a relative lack of self-disclosure by clients on offense-related themes was expected. Other differences included the perceived agency roles (e.g., "education and assistance" from nonstatutory services vs. "reform and rehabilitation" from social work services).

Behavioral Measures

The same range of measures was used at baseline and follow-up to measure the impact of AECs on client behaviors. These measures were identical to those used in other locations. The MSI was used throughout for baseline interviews, and in conjunction with the collateral interview at follow-up.

Results

A total of 356 clients were identified by the Perth courts; 18 were successfully interviewed for a baseline assessment, whose mean age was 21.9 years (range 16.6–28.3 years).

TABLE 7.1. Summary Data of Perth/Forfar AEC Study.

	Perth (Control group)		Forfar (Information-based AEC)	
	Baseline	Follow-up	Baseline	Follow-up
1.	31.7	31.6	47.9	32.5
2.	2.2	1.6	3.2	2.0
3.	94.6	98.2	53.9	101.3
4.	5.5	4.0	3.7	4.2
5.	19.9	22.4	15.4	22.2
6.	6.9	3.2	4.2	3.1
7.	2.7	0.8	2.0	0.5
8.	8.7	9.9	20.0	26.0
9.	64.9	84.6	80.8	82.2
10.	17.9	9.5	9.8	9.7
11.	6.5	1.5	0.6	0.8
12.	12.4	2.4	1.7	1.9
13.	3.5	0.3	0.7	0.8
14.	6.5	3.0	3.6	3.9
15.	11.2	7.7	7.1	7.9
16.	22.3	13.2	15.4	11.3

1. mean number of units per week; 2. average number of drinking sessions per week; 3. mean number of units in "heavy drinking week"; 4. mean number of sessions in "heavy drinking week"; 5. mean number of units in "heavy drinking session"; 6. mean number of "life problems"(alcohol-related and nonalcohol-related); 7. mean number of "life problems"(alcohol-related only); 8. mean ideal drinking level (units per week); 9. mean percentage confidence ratings; 10. mean SADQ values; 11. mean number of offenses against property (self-reported); 12. mean number of offenses against rules and regulations (self-reported); 13. mean number of offenses against other persons (self-reported); 14. mean values MAST; 15. mean values Attitudes to Drinking Questionnaire; 16. mean values General Health Questionnaire.

From the Forfar courts, 20 clients were referred and completed an AEC baseline assessment with a mean age of 20.3 years (range 18.3–22.9 years). (See Table 7.1.).

Two-way analysis of variance produced several significantly different interaction effects. Specifically, significantly different effects ($p \leq .05$) were obtained on (a) all life problems, Perth (6.9 to 3.2) and Forfar (4.2 to 3.1), although preintervention levels of life problems were significantly higher among the Perth control group ($p \leq .05$).

Significantly different effects were also observed on (b) property offenses ($p \leq .05$) Perth (8.6 to 0.4) and Forfar (0.7 to 0.3), (c) rules offenses ($p \leq .05$) Perth (14.3 to 3.0) and Forfar (1.8 to 1.1), (d) person offenses ($p \leq .05$) Perth (6.5 to 0.4) and Forfar (0.8 to 0.8), and (e) MAST scores ($p \leq .01$) Perth (6.5 to 3.4) and Forfar (3.9 to 3.6). On (c) to (e), however, the preintervention scores in the Perth group were all significantly higher than the Forfar group ($p \leq .05$).

Preintervention between-groups comparisons of the Perth (control group) and Forfar (experimental group) produced several significant differences. They were (a) units in a "heavy" drinking week, (b) life problems, (c) ideal levels of drinking, (d) self-reported offenses against property, (e) self-reported offenses against rules, (f) self-reported offenses against persons, and (g) prior history of incarceration.

Specifically, the Perth group drank more in a "heavy" week (95 units compared to 54 units in Forfar); they also reported more life problems than the Forfar group (6.9 compared to 4.2); the Forfar group selected a higher ideal drinking goal (20 units per week compared to 9). The Perth group had a higher number of self-reported offenses in all three categories of offense (property, rules and person) (t tests, p ≤ .05 in each case). Moreover, control group subjects were more likely to have been incarcerated (94%) than experimental subjects (30%) (p ≤ .001). Finally, 66% of control group subjects were wine drinkers, compared with 20% of experimental subjects (p ≤ .05).

While control and experimental groups did not differ in preintervention measures on the dependent variables (e.g., conviction rate, drinking behavior), there were initial differences on some specific variables. In summary, the spectrum of clients in the control group may have been a more "chronic" population, with regard to some of their drinking and offending behaviors.

Follow-up data were reported for 13 (72%) clients in the control group (mean follow-up time, 18 months) (range 6–21 months). Thirteen (65%) clients completed a follow-up in the experimental group (mean follow-up time, 16 months) (range 11–17 months).

Comparisons were made between subjects who completed an AEC and follow-up interview with subjects who completed an AEC and dropped out of the study following AEC completion. There were three statistical differences between the two groups. First, in the follow-up group the mean age of school leaving was lower (15.6 years) than in the "drop out" group (16.2 years) (p ≤ .05 years). The "follow-up" group had a higher ideal drinking limit (26.8 units) than the "drop out" group (9.0 units) (p ≤ .05, t test). In the "follow-up" group 2/11 were not wine drinkers compared with 9/11 in the "drop out" group (chi-square, (p ≤ .05).

Analysis of Change at Follow-Up

Between-groups comparisons of control/experimental AEC outcome data produced no significant differences on any variables (t test independent samples).

Examination of the within-group differences of the control group at baseline and follow-up produced several significant statistical differences. These included: (a) a significant reduction in "life problems" (6.9 to 3.2) (p ≤ .001), (b) increased confidence ratings about reaching ideal drinking levels (64.9% to 84.6%) (p ≤ .05), (c) a significant reduction in self-reported offenses against rules and regulations (12.3 to 2.4) (p ≤ .05), (d) a significant reduction in offenses against other persons (3.5 to 0.3) (p ≤ .05), and (e) a significant reduction in MAST scores (6.4 to 3.0) (p ≤ .01) (t tests, related samples).

Within-group differences of the information-based AEC at baseline and follow-up produced a significant reduction in the average number of units drunk per week (47.9 to 32.5) (p ≤ .001)(t tests, matched-pairs test). A significant reduction in average numbers of drinking sessions per week also was observed (3.2 to 2) (p ≤ .001). Also, a significant reduction in average number of "alcohol-related life problems" was observed in the information based group (2.0 to 0.5) (p ≤ .05). Also, units consumed in a "heavy" week increased from 54 to 101 (p ≤ .05).

Collateral Interviews

There were no significant differences in agreement between the collateral groups in the Perth and Forfar populations at follow-up (chi-square test). In Perth, 11/12 collaterals agreed on levels of drinking and 10/11 agreed on subsequent levels of offending behavior. In Forfar, there was agreement from 6/11 collaterals on drinking and 9/10 on levels of offending.

In addition to these differences of within-group change between baseline and follow-up, several trends emerged that indicated statistically nonsignificant but clinically relevant modifications in drinking/offending behavior.

Combined Analysis

The data from all studies were pooled to determine effects of interactions between interventions and time effects. This required comparisons between (a) talk-based AECs (Dundee and Glasgow), (b) behavioral AECs (Dundee and Glasgow), (c) information-based AECs (Forfar), and (d) no-intervention control group (Perth).

Two-way analysis of variance revealed significantly different interaction effects on property offenses and rules/regulations offenses.

Property offenses (e.g., housebreaking):

—talk-based AECs decrease (1.0 to 0.3) (p ≤ .05)
—behavioral AECs decrease (3.1 to 2.5) (p ≤ .05)
—information-based AECs decrease (0.7 to 0.3) (p ≤ .05)
—no-intervention control decrease (8.6 to 0.4) (p ≤ .05)

These results were explained by differences in effects in the Perth/Forfar study (p ≤ .05). No other pairs of groups revealed significantly different interaction effects.

Rules offenses (e.g., riding on a bus without a ticket; not paying fines):

—talk-based AECs decrease (6.8 to 3.0) (p ≤ .005)
—behavioral AECs increase (4.4 to 6.4) (p ≤ .005)
—information-based AECs decrease (1.8 to 1.1) (p ≤ .005)
—no-intervention control decrease (14.3 to 3.0) (p ≤ .005)

These differences are explained by differences in effect in comparisons between behavioral AECs and no-intervention control (p ≤ .005), and no-intervention control and information-based AECs (p ≤ .05).

Significant differences, however, were found on this variable on precourse ANOVA. The information-based AEC (Forfar) and behavioral AEC (Dundee/Glasgow) were found to differ significantly from the no-intervention control group (Perth).

Examination of precourse quantitative data between groups produced several significant differences, including those listed below.

Ideal drinking levels (units per week): the behavioral AEC group (Dundee/Glasgow) (9.5) and no-intervention control group (8.7) each differed significantly (p ≤ .05) from the information-based AEC group (20.0) (one-way ANOVA).

Rules/regulations offenses: the behavioral AEC group (Dundee/Glasgow) (4.4) and the information-based AEC group (Forfar) (1.7) each differed significantly (p ≤ .05, one-way ANOVA) from the no-intervention control group (Perth) (12.4).

Examination of between-groups precourse qualitative data also produced several significant differences, including:

Incarceration: twelve out of 13 clients in the no-intervention control group (Perth) had been previously incarcerated (p ≤ .001; chi-square test).

Wine drinking: ten out of 13 clients in the no-intervention control group (Perth) were wine drinkers (p ≤ .05; chi-square test).

Drinking location: seven out of 10 clients in the behavioral AEC groups (Dundee/Glasgow) drank alcohol from "carry outs" (i.e., off-licence stores); most other clients drank alcohol mainly in pubs/clubs (p ≤ .05; chi-square test).

Examination of the postcourse quantitative data between groups produced one significant difference on number of life problems:

Life problems: the no-intervention control group (Perth) 6.9 and the information-based AEC group differed significantly (p ≤ .05) from the talk-based AEC group (3.1) (one-way ANOVA).

Examination of the postcourse qualitative data between groups produced one significant difference in drinking styles:

Controlled drinking: eight out of 13 clients in the information-based AEC group had never tried controlled drinking (p ≤ .005; chi-square test).

Examination of qualitative data from between-group comparisons at baseline and follow-up did not produce statistically significant differences, with the exception of (a) incarceration of clients 11/13 Perth, 5/13 Forfar, (p ≤ .05) and (b) married clients 4/13 Perth, 0/13 Forfar (p ≤ .05).

Discussion

Interpretation of the research data is confounded by the initial nonequivalence of the two research populations. No differences were found between the Perth and Forfar populations on the main dependent variables (conviction rates, drinking behavior). Other initial differences, however, suggest that the Perth (control) population had been recruited from a client group with more chronic problems (Baldwin, Gamba, Heather, Lawson, & Robertson, 1991).

The large differences in referral base rates (Perth n = 356; Forfar n = 20) may have indicated that referral agents (i.e., sheriffs) were applying different criteria in their selection procedures. Examination of their actual practice in both courts, however, did not corroborate this explanation.

First, examination of court lists indicated a greater overall volume of work in the Perth Sheriff Courts. For example, the volume was sufficient to generate enough work for two full-time sheriffs and not one as in Forfar.

Second, the impact of making referral for a "control group" was different to the impact of making referral for an alcohol education course. In particular, it would be expected that whereas all sheriffs applied the same criteria, the Perth sheriffs would be more likely to identify clients eligible for the control group because this procedure would have no tariff or consequences in the courts.

Thus, while Perth sheriffs were required to apply identical criteria to identify eligible clients, there was no additional work involved or legal consequences in the courts. In contrast, identification of eligible candidates in Forfar (and other AEC locations) produced considerable administrative work for the court. (Each referral, for example, required at least a doubling of the court lists as well as administrative processing of the referral letter, report, and recommendations.)

Several factors may have interacted to produce a situation of unequal referral rates between the two courts. One effect of the low response rate from the total Perth population ($18/356 = 5\%$) would have been to influence the sample representativeness. Clients who responded to the initial recruitment letter by agreeing to participate in the research evaluation may have been nonrepresentative of the overall population, differing in characteristics such as problem severity, motivation to change, and "readiness" for adaptive change. In addition, the imposition of strict entry criteria into the study restricted the generalizability of the findings (Kraemer, 1981).

One implication of these observed preintervention differences in initial measures of specific characteristics might be that some observed follow-up differences between the two groups may be explained by regression effects. Specifically, changes between different assessment occasions would be due to a reversion of scores toward the mean. (These probabilities may be even higher in a research population of young offenders, who tend to score at the extreme on initial measures.)

Similar follow-up rates between the two groups ($65\%/72\%$) suggest that observed differences may not be attributable to differences in attrition due to population characteristics; these percentages also are consistent with follow-up rates obtained in forensic populations (e.g., Spence, 1979). The attrition rates ($35\%/28\%$), however, exceeded those obtained in similar intervention/control studies with other client populations ($11\%/9\%$) from meta-analyses of outcome research (Shapiro & Shapiro, 1983). The high client attrition may have introduced bias in comparisons between groups. Equally, a high completion rate of follow-up interviews after long intervals ($x = 16$ months) suggests that follow-up data might be representative of the overall population and also that any effects obtained might be durable. Nonetheless, differential attrition rates in a quasi-experimental study distort efforts to estimate statistically and control the potential influence of client variables (Howard, Krause, & Orlinsky, 1986).

The within-group differences observed in the control group suggests that several processes (otherwise attributable to main effects) could be a function of time effects (i.e., so-called spontaneous remission). In particular, the reduction in "life problems" indicates that some improvement in other areas not related to alcohol may occur as a function of age or a secondary consequence of other "life events" (e.g., marriage, housing, or employment). The observed regulations and property, however, suggest a rival explanation.

Specifically, subject improvement in the control condition may have been attributable to reactive experimental arrangements: subjects may have been influenced in their awareness that they were participating in a special program. Equally, the improvement may be attributable to reactive assessment: subjects' awareness of assessments of their behavior may have influenced their response (e.g., Bernstein, 1973; Kazdin, 1978). It may also indicate some possible benefits of "assessment only" screening interventions with such clients.

The within-group differences observed in the behavioral group, however, suggests that some alterations in drinking behavior occurred that did not occur in the control group. These included reductions in numbers of units drunk per week and in number of drinking sessions per week. As in the control group, a reduction in "other life problems" occurred, which supports an hypothesis that some observed reductions in both groups could be attributable to time effects or reactivity effects.

Examination of Table 7.1 confirmed that while the information-based AEC produced a reduction (47.9 to 32.5) of units drunk per week, where the control group did not produce this effect (31.7 to 31.6), the information-based AEC produced a higher average number of units drunk during a "heavy drinking week" (53.9 to 101.3) than the control group, which remained constant (94.6 to 98.2). This indicates that when the information-based AEC group relapsed into heavy drinking, their drinking levels during the relapse episode exceeded both their previous levels and the levels of the control group. Both control group and the information-based AEC group produced similar average follow-up levels during a "heavy drinking session" (22.4 and 22.1). Both groups also produced similar follow-up levels of "other life problems" (3.2 and 3.1). Both groups reported similar follow-up "confidence ratings" in their ability to stick to ideal drinking levels (84.6% and 82.2%).

The control group reported average reductions in offending behavior in all three categories: property 6.4 to 1.5; rules and regulations 12.4 to 2.4; persons 3.5 to 0.3. In contrast, the information-based AEC reported increases in offending behaviors in all three categories: property 0.6 to 0.8; rules and regulations 1.7 to 1.9; persons 0.7 to 0.8. These results support the hypothesis that some improvement in offending rates might be expected as a result of reactive experimental arrangements (or reactive assessment) in the control group.

Paradoxically, however, one effect of attendance at an information-based AEC may be to precipitate future offending behavior, despite similar effects from reactive assessment and reactive experimental arrangements. Examination of self-reported questionnaires suggested reductions in MAST and GHQ values and improved attitudes to drinking in the control group; in the information-based AEC group, increases were found in MAST and GHQ values and deteriorated attitudes to drinking.

Use of this intervention-control study is subject to criticisms of all control group studies. Specifically, ethical questions should be raised following deprivation of clients from a potentially effective intervention. Also, practical problems were created from keeping nonintervention clients within the study and away from other forms of help (Basham, 1986). In addition, the threat of "expectancy artifacts" (i.e., the development of condition-specific expectancies by clients about likely improvement) remained unresolved. The effect of demand artifacts on the clients in the control condition may have influenced outcome and inflated estimates of effectiveness.

Summary

Unresolved problems of design may have exerted limits on statistical validity, power, feasibility, and clinical value. Subsequent studies could be improved with use of intensive designs (e.g., Kraemer, 1981), although there are associated analytical problems.

Specifically, while an information-based AEC reduced weekly drinking to levels comparable to those in a control population, it may reverse effects in other aspects of drinking behavior (e.g., *increase* in drinking levels during a period of relapse). Also, an information-based AEC may have an unwanted effect on offending rates: specifically, this type of intervention may precipitate further offending.

These results do not support the use of information-based AECs in preference to a no-intervention control group involving assessment only interviews. Use of an information-based AEC did not achieve results improved on no-intervention control at 16 months follow-up. In addition, use of "assessment only," screening interviews may have useful prophylactic effects on drinking/offending behaviors.

8
Noranside

Previous studies were completed in noninstitutional settings using referral systems established with local courts. In the United Kingdom, many AEC services have been established in local settings (Gamba et al., 1989), and many similar services have been provided in corrections institutions (McGill, Williamson, Roberts, & Frith, 1987; McMurran & Baldwin, 1989). To date, however, none has been evaluated; prisons and young offender institutions have continued to provide AEC services in the absence of any supporting data on effectiveness.

The study was based in a young offenders institution 10 miles north of Forfar. It was an open institution with places for 390 male inmates. The YOI social worker had made a request for alcohol education following repeated requests from inmates; more than 50% of inmates interviewed at admission had indicated alcohol as a factor in their offense behaviors.

Initial discussions were completed with the social worker about the possible implementation of an AEC program in the institution. Formal agreement was obtained from the YOI governor and further assistance was requested from other disciplines. Specifically, agreement was reached with the education department and prison psychologist to assist in the establishment and maintenance of an AEC service for prerelease young offenders. This approach was consistent with guidelines for behavioral interventions in penal institutions (Rizvi, Hyland, & Blackstock, 1984). It was also designed to minimize system barriers to institutional reforms by making services directly available to offender/client populations (Iglehart & Stein, 1985).

The focus on prerelease young offenders was based on the rationale that inmates most likely to benefit from educational interventions were those persons waiting for discharge: potential new learning might be maximized by recency effects. A main hypothesis of the experimental design was that differences would be found between the two groups of offender/clients at follow-up. This was based on the premise that the "active ingredients" of AECs would be the acquisition of behavioral skills and the progressive "shaping" and refinement of these techniques, via AEC feedback sessions. It was hypothesized that without this behavioral feedback and the opportunity to rehearse new skills, new learning would be minimal.

Experimental Hypothesis

The experimental hypothesis suggested that differences would be found at follow-up between the behavioral AEC and no-intervention control groups: limited opportunities to develop an appropriate skills repertoire (e.g., self-monitoring, target setting, drink diary records) via rehearsal would enable the modification of problem behaviors (i.e., drinking/offending).

Method

Experimental Design

The YOI study was a true experimental evaluation design with random allocation of subjects to a no-intervention control group. This design was used to examine the random effects of naturally occurring events in the environments of young offenders released from a corrections institution.

The experimental group completed a behavioral AEC with six weekly sessions of 2 hours each. The control group did not receive an AEC (nor any other alcohol education materials) and attended their usual institutional activities (e.g., work details) while the experimental group attended the AEC. (Participants of the AEC were diverted from their usual work routines for 2 hours to attend the course.)

Independent Variable

The independent variable was presence or absence of the behavioral AEC.

Dependent Variables

The experimental design included two main dependent variables: (a) drinking behavior and (b) offending behavior. The main hypothesis was that differences would be found between the experimental and control groups.

None of the previous studies included random allocation of subjects to experimental and control groups, due to local constraints on design. Provision of an AEC service in an institutional setting offered the opportunity to implement the preferred design, based on the inclusion of a no-intervention control group. Possible objections on ethical grounds were anticipated. The use of a no-intervention control group was not problematic, however, as AEC services had remained unevaluated. Continued provision of unevaluated services may have been more ethically questionable than the introduction of a no-intervention control group (West, 1980).

The design was based on random allocation of offender/clients to an experimental (behavioral AEC) or control (no-intervention) group.

Subjects

Specific criteria were used to identify the potential client population within the YOI. Self-referrals were encouraged for clients who:

1. were aged between 17 and 21 years
2. stated they would attend for an AEC interview
3. had committed 2 or more offenses
4. had more than half of their total offenses alcohol-related.

Materials

The contents of this institutional AEC were similar to the original AEC model, with omissions of some context-inappropriate material (e.g., it was not possible for offender/clients to rehearse the skills of controlled drinking between AEC sessions).

The institutional AEC sessions included:

SESSION ONE: INTRODUCTION

—contracting for attendance (Stuart, 1971)
—self-recording of drinking behavior (Robertson & Heather, 1985)
—"Sensible Drinking" video (Baldwin et al., 1988)
—drinking analysis questionnaires (Robertson & Heather, 1985)
—drink diaries (SHEG, 1985a)

SESSION TWO: ALCOHOL AND SELF-MONITORING

—review contract
—"units of alcohol" concept
—"That's the Limit" booklet (HEC, 1985)
—alcohol and physical health acetate pack (Baldwin et al., 1988)
—dangerous/risky/safer drinking levels
—"The Enjoyable Limit" video (SCA, 1985a)
—setting personal limits for drinking
—task assignment

SESSION THREE: DRINKING AND OFFENDING

—review progress
—"tolerance" discussion
—drinking/driving discussion
—"Saturday Night/Sunday Morning" video (SHEG, 1985b)
—personal drinking rules
—exploring personal offending behavior (McGuire & Priestley, 1985)

SESSION FOUR: PERSONAL VALUES AND OFFENDING—I

—review progress
—offense severity exercise
—reasons for and against crime (McGuire & Priestley, 1985)
—choosing appropriate role models exercise

SESSION FIVE: PERSONAL VALUES AND OFFENDING—II

—review progress
—reasons for offending and for not offending exercise
—"The Victim Experience" trigger video (Baldwin et al., 1988)
—assertion skills exercise (McGuire & Priestley, 1985)
—effects of heavy/moderate drinking styles

SESSION SIX: PREVENTING REOFFENDING

—review progress
—drinking analysis questionnaire
—decision-making exercise (McGuire & Priestley, 1985)
—self-monitoring skills exercise (Stumphauzer, 1986)
—self-control skills exercise (Stumphauzer, 1986)
—review AEC
—contract follow-up interview appointment

(based on the "Alcohol Education Course for Young Offenders in Secure Settings" [Baldwin, Wilson, Lancaster, Allsop, McGowan, McMurran & Hodge, 1989]).

Procedure

Offender/clients were identified for the AEC research study via examination of their institutional records. A cohort of eligible inmates was identified whose release date was between 6 and 8 weeks in the future. These people were invited to participate in a research study.

Each member of the group (n = 27) was approached individually by the social worker or teacher at the YOI. The following rationale was presented to the offender:

> You have made a request for some assistance with your drinking. We would like to help you with this, and we may be able to offer you the opportunity to join an alcohol education course. We would like to interview you to see if you would fit into the course. There are, however, limited places, and it may not be possible to offer you assistance, even if you are eligible. Would you still like to be interviewed for an Alcohol Education Course?

All offenders agreed to be interviewed and the MSI was completed by the social worker, prison psychologist, or teacher. All interviewed offenders were found to be eligible, according to the original criteria (i.e., aged between 17 and 21 years; stated they would like to attend an AEC; had committed two or more offenses; had more than half their total offenses alcohol-related).

Motivational Screening Interviews

An MSI was given to all offenders in experimental and control groups; this was completed by the social worker, teacher, or prison psychologist. Each professional had achieved criterion performance with the MSI; particular attention was given to sections on collateral information. Some MSI sections (e.g., drinking in past 7 days) were inapplicable and therefore omitted.

Completion of the MSI was complemented by a description to clients of the rationale for an AEC. This contained the following statements:

> You have been interviewed for an alcohol education course because you feel there might be a relationship between your drinking and offending behavior. We have discussed this, and it seems to me that there is (not) a relationship between your drinking and getting into trouble with the police. Some/most/every time(s) you have been arrested or jailed, you had been drinking, is that correct?
>
> If you decide to join an alcohol education course, this is how it works. There is no pressure for you to attend an alcohol education course. In fact, the opposite: if you feel you are here under obligation, I suggest you do not attend. I'm really only interested in working with people who want to do something about their drinking and getting into trouble. I think if you feel under pressure to attend, the course is not for you: you should only attend if you are wanting to sort out your problems.
>
> What do you think? Do you think the course might be helpful to you?

The function of this section was to clarify to the offender/client that responsibility for change was their own decision: paradoxical statements were used to convey to the client that they should make their own personal decision.

All clients who completed an MSI expressed an interest in attending an AEC. This was unsurprising, as clients had self-selected themselves for an initial interview and were highly motivated to attend. AEC procedures were explained to all clients, specifically that regular and punctual attendance was expected and that weekly assignments should be completed as required.

> You will be starting your alcohol education course next week. One condition of attending is that we would like to interview you again 6 months after you leave. Do you still wish to join the course?

The control group members were informed:

> Unfortunately, it will not be possible for you to join the alcohol education course, as there are insufficient spaces. We would, however, still like to interview you again 6 months after you leave, to see how you are doing.

All offenders agreed to be interviewed and signed consent forms indicating their willingness to participate in the study. They were assured confidentiality during the course and at follow-up interviews.

Alcohol Education Course Presentation

The AEC was similar to the delivery in the original study. Materials were presented so that offender/clients could acquire information and/or skills. Explicit attempts at teaching were rare; instead, attempts were made to set the conditions for learning. An atmosphere of trust was promoted, with clear guidelines about confidentiality and membership.

AEC standardization of delivery was difficult, although individual styles of presentation were specified where possible. Similar to the original study some styles were proscribed (authoritative or directive) while others (supportive and facilitative) were encouraged (Heron, 1975).

Support System for Alcohol Education Courses

Establishment of AECs within corrections settings was consistent with national initiatives (McMurran & Baldwin, 1989). None of these other services, however, had included a controlled evaluation design to measure effectiveness. The study was the first attempt at AEC service provision using a no-intervention control group: robust supports were required to implement this system.

Initial discussions with the YOI governor indicated that institution staff might participate in future AEC service provision. In the interim, however, an independent support system for AEC services was required, which did not rely on prison officer involvement.

Teaching and training sessions were scheduled with the prison psychologist, teacher, and social worker to complete the MSI to criterion performance (i.e., completion in less than 50 minutes, full documentation of drinking/offending behaviors, self-report data, data for follow-up contact). In addition, the social worker and teacher observed behavioral AECs and subsequently participated as co-tutors with AEC session materials. Both persons then presented AECs as tutors with other staff as nonparticipant observers.

The provision of AECs at the YOI also was based on a multilevel model of implementation: (a) direct services for clients (interviews/AECs), (b) in-service training for YOI staff (teacher/social worker/prison officers), and (c) system developments (e.g., meetings with governor) to promote maintenance of services.

Behavioral Measures

A range of measures was used to examine the impact of behavioral AEC/no-intervention on drinking and offending behaviors.

Baseline

At initial interview, the MSI was used to obtain data on drinking and offending behaviors. In addition, clients were requested to complete Drinking Attitudes Questionnaire, MAST, SADQ, GHQ, and the Offenses Questionnaire.

Data on drinking behavior were obtained from two self-report drinking windows: "drinking on 7 days prior to incarceration" and "period of heavy drinking during 6 months before incarceration." Data on offending behavior were obtained from "self-reported offenses since first recorded offense" to date of incarceration. Clients signed consent forms to acknowledge their participation.

Follow-Up

All offender/clients were informed they would be contacted 12 months following discharge from the institution. Information about collateral source also was identified at the initial interview.

Clients were contacted by letter or by telephone 12 months after discharge and were offered five pounds for completion of the interview. Follow-up interviews were completed by research workers "blind" to the experimental hypothesis.

Collateral Interviews

In addition to data obtained during baseline and follow-up interviews, information also was required from other sources to corroborate (or disconfirm) this clinical perspective. Consent was obtained from the client for this interview which was completed by direct contact or by telephone. Collateral interviews also were completed with spouses, drinking partners, best friends, or relatives.

Results

A total of 14 offender/clients with a mean age of 19.4 years (range 16.9 -20.8 years) completed a behavioral AEC; 13 were included in a control group (assessment only) (range 17.5–22.4 years) of clients with a mean age of 19.4 years. Between-group comparisons of behavioral AEC/control group data at baseline produced no quantitative differences, with one exception: subjects in the experimental group had a significantly greater average number of property offenses (n = 21) than subjects in the control group (n = 4) (p ≤ .05, t test, independent samples). No qualitative differences were found between the two groups, with one exception: subjects in the control group were more likely to report drinking in pubs and clubs; in contrast, subjects in the experimental group were more likely to report drinking from "carry outs" in public places (p ≤ .05, chi-square test).

Follow-Up Rates

Follow-up rates are reported for 7 (60%) clients in the control group (mean follow-up time, 14 months; range 9–21 months) and for 14 (100%) clients in the experimental group (mean follow-up time, 14 months; range 12–18 months).

Comparisons were made between subjects who completed an AEC and a follow-up interview with subjects who completed an AEC and dropped out of the study following AEC completion. There were two statistical differences between the two groups. In the "follow-up" group, the mean number of drinking sessions in a heavy drinking week was less (2.5 per week) than in the "dropout" group (4.7

per week) (p ≤ .05); t test). Also, in the "follow-up" group 19/21 clients were not wine drinkers, compared with 1/6 in the "dropout" group (p ≤ .005, chi-square).

Analysis of Change at Follow-Up

Two-way analysis of variance produced several significantly different interaction effects. Specifically: (a) the control group increased average number of units per week (123 to 140), whereas the AEC group decreased units per week (140 to 63), (b) the control group increased average units per drinking session (21 to 43), whereas the AEC group decreased (27 to 18), (c) the control group (4.2–5.9) increased number of offenses against property, whereas the AEC group decreased (21.2–4.6), (d) both control group (20 to 18) and AEC group (20 to 5.6) reduced the number of "rules offenses" (two-way ANOVA; p ≤ .05).

Between-groups comparisons of behavioral AEC/control group outcome data produced significant differences on several variables: (a) behavioral AEC subjects self-reported less drinking in average number of units per session (18 units) compared with the no-intervention control group (43 units) (p ≤ .05), (b) behavioral AEC subjects average self-reported offenses against "rules and regulations" (5.1 offenses) compared with the no-intervention control group (19 offenses) (p ≤ .05), (c) behavioral AEC subjects average self-reported offenses against persons (1 offense) compared with no-intervention control group (2.7 offenses) (p ≤ .05) (t tests, independent samples).

Comparison of the within-group differences of the behavioral AEC group at baseline and follow-up produced significant reductions in several domains, including: (a) a significant reduction in average number of alcohol-related problems (6 to 2) (p ≤ .05), (b) decrease in offenses against "rules and regulations" (20 to 5) (p ≤ .005), (c) decrease in offenses against persons (8 to 1) (p ≤ .01), (d) decrease in Attitudes to Drinking Questionnaire scores (14 to 9) (p ≤ .05), (e) significant increases in ideal average weekly drinking levels (12.4 to 27.1 units per week) (p ≤ .05), and (f) increase in expressed confidence levels for adhering to stated limits on drinking (50% to 95%) (p ≤ .001)(t tests, related samples).

Comparison of the within-group differences of the no-intervention control group at baseline and follow-up produced no significant differences.

Collateral Interviews

No significant differences were found between control and experimental groups for collateral reports (chi-square tests). In the control group 5/6 collaterals agreed on levels of drinking and 6/6 on levels of offending behavior. In the experimental group, 10/12 collaterals agreed on levels of drinking and 11/12 on levels of offending behavior.

Differences of within-group change between baseline and follow-up are summarized in Table 8.1.

TABLE 8.1. Summary Data of Noranside AEC Study.

	Control group		Behavioral AEC	
	Baseline	Follow-up	Baseline	Follow-up
1.	123	210	140	63
2.	21	43	27	18
3.	155	262	152	143
4.	33	45	30	28
5.	4.3	2.8	3.4	2.3
6.	5.3	6.4	7.4	5.4
7.	4.1	4.0	5.9	2.3
8.	4.2	5.9	21.2	4.6
9.	20	19	20	5.1
10.	5.0	2.7	8.3	1.0
11.	11.4	11.6	14.1	8.6
12.	20.4	12.4	24.8	14.6

1. mean number of units per week; 2. average number of units per drinking session; 3. mean number of units ("heavy drinking period"); 4. mean number of units per session during "heavy drinking period"; 5. conviction rates (self-reported); 6. mean number of "life problems"; 7. mean number of "life problems" (alcohol-related only); 8. mean number of offenses against property (self-reported); 9. mean number of offenses against rules and regulations (self-reported); 10. mean number of offenses against persons (self-reported); 11. mean values Attitudes to Drinking Questionnaire; 12. mean values General Health Questionnaire.

Discussion

The results of the study are limited by the failure to obtain a required minimum number of subjects for both intervention and control conditions. Such studies ideally should not fall below a sample size of 10 subjects per condition (Kraemer, 1981). Despite the limitations imposed by small sizes, however, some trends have emerged. There is some support for the rejection of the null hypothesis: data obtained support the rival hypothesis that the experimental intervention (behavioral AEC) impacted on both drinking and offending behaviors. Follow-up differences on both dependent variables were found in the experimental group but not the control group.

An overall follow-up rate of 80% was obtained at an average of 14 months after initial baseline measures. Some differences between percentages of successful follow-ups between groups was observed; despite a successful completion of follow-up interviews with 21 of the original 27 clients, some of the observed effects may be due to differential attrition between the two groups. Nonetheless, 60% completion of follow-up interviews does not necessarily suggest the follow-up sample population was unrepresentative.

Another threat to external validity might have been the reactivity of the research context. Specifically, subjects may have been influenced by an awareness that they were participating in a special program: subjects may have behaved differently, depending on the reactivity of the intervention and the program to which they were exposed. In addition, specific behaviors studied in applied research may vary in topography and qualitative characteristics from the clinical problems to which results might be generalized (Kazdin, 1978).

Notwithstanding these methodological limitations, reductions in both dependent variables (drinking and offending behaviors) were achieved as main effects of the study. In particular, the behavioral AEC exerted an effect to reduce self-reported drinking behavior at follow-up, while control group subjects had increased their drinking during the same period. Similar reductions were observed in number of units per drinking session and mean number of units per week during heavy drinking period. In sum, the impact of a behavioral AEC on a prerelease group of incarcerated young offenders produced some durable significant reductions in drinking behavior (Baldwin, Greer, Heather, Robb, Robertson, Ward, & Williams, 1991).

In addition, the behavioral AEC also impacted on (self-reported) offending behavior. (While self-reported conviction rates were uncorroborated, offender/clients were aware of potential access by the researchers to court data and police records). Other studies have suggested that offender/client self-report data can be highly reliable. In the experimental group, statistically significant reductions were obtained in self-reported offenses against rules and regulations, property, and persons; whereas both control group and experimental group subjects reported a decrease in overall offending rates, control group subjects reported a specific (nonsignificant) decrease only in offenses against persons.

In sum, while some reductions in self-reported offending rates would be expected from reactivity effects, the impact of a behavioral AEC on a released group of young offenders produced significant reductions in some offending behaviors at follow-up. These reductions were not observed in a control group that did not receive an AEC. In addition to significant follow-up differences in the main dependent variables between control and experimental groups, other statistically significant differences were observed.

In the behavioral AEC group at follow-up, significant reductions were observed in the number of alcohol-related problems, together with reductions in average SADQ scores. Significant improvements in Attitudes to Drinking scores were noted, as well as increases in ideal average weekly drinking level (which might suggest a more realistic target level of drinking). These changes were complemented by a significant increase in confidence levels in achieving personal drinking targets. These differences were not obtained in the control group, which suggests that these complementary improvements may have been achieved as secondary, indirect effects of behavioral AEC implementation.

Examination of the follow-up data suggest that, while behavioral AEC subjects had reduced volume alcohol intake at follow-up, average levels of drinking still exceeded the limits of "safer" drinking (i.e., 63 units, which exceeds a "safer" drinking level by a factor of 3). This finding raised the question of clinical significance of the results: even this 55% reduction of average drinking levels might be considered insufficient if most clients continued to drink alcohol at levels beyond "safer" limits. Similarly, reductions in sessional levels of drinking from 27 to 18 units represents a statistically significant improvement; "clinical improvement" might be jeopardized, however, by an average session level (18 units) highly likely to produce regular intoxications.

In addition, during periods of heavy drinking ("relapse episodes") offender/clients who had completed a behavioral AEC continued to drink at very dangerous intake levels (e.g., 143 units average). Despite the achievement of significant statistical improvements not found in the control group, this confirmed that clinical improvement may not have been sufficient to avoid further risk from alcohol-related problems.

Nonetheless, one interpretation of between-groups follow-up data is that completion of a behavioral AEC may inoculate against further deterioration in drinking behavior and alcohol-related problems: in the no-intervention control group, increases were observed between baseline and follow-up in several domains, including mean number of units per week (123–210), average number of units per drinking session (21–43), mean number of units per week ("heavy drinking period") (155–262), mean number of units per session during "heavy drinking period" (33–45), and mean number of other life problems (5.3–6.4).

The non-achievement of an adequate sample size in both conditions is a barrier to the generality of the results; one or two offender/clients with extreme scores may have dominated the results obtained. In addition, with fewer than 10 in the sample, odds favor finding nonsignificant results, even if effects have been obtained (Kraemer, 1981).

The observed differences between experimental (AEC) and control (no-intervention) groups provides some evidence to support rejection of the null hypothesis. Despite the absence of opportunities for offender/clients to rehearse skills related to controlled drinking/abstinence and "not offending" between sessions, exposure to therapeutic materials during sessions exerted a positive effect on subsequent behavior. (For example, while behavioral AEC offender/clients were not able to keep a drinking diary during the course, many people expressed the intention to complete a drink diary after release). Equally, exposure to therapeutic materials and group discussions of specific topics may have increased the probability of positive decision making in the group about specific "reform behaviors" (e.g., "When I am released, I will not hang around with Billy and Dave," or "After I leave here, I am going to stick to my drinking levels").

Summary

Although generalizations beyond this population are restricted by the methodological limitations of the study, completion of a behavioral AEC by prerelease incarcerated offenders may reduce some drinking and offending behaviors in the medium term.

9

Kilmarnock

Background

The controlled evaluation of effectiveness of AECs was based on four independent but related studies in Dundee (five), Glasgow (six), Perth/Forfar (seven), and Noranside (eight).

Studies in Dundee, Perth, Forfar, and Glasgow all were established on a system of referral from the District or Sheriff Courts; eligible candidates for AECs were referred from the courts for assessment interviews to the local Council on Alcohol or Social Work Department.

Throughout the evaluation research project, one factor limited the development of services in each setting where AECs were established. With the exception of Perth (where eligible candidates were identified for a "control" group only) the growth of all other AEC services was restricted by the same factor: low referral base rates.

Dundee

The Scottish alcohol/offending evaluation project was established in Dundee during 1985 in a local climate of relative optimism and enthusiasm for interventions with teenagers and young adult offenders.

Referral criteria for AEC initial MSIs had been specified and court officials had been notified of the new service. Despite the establishment of several procedures to inform and educate users of the local Sheriff and District Courts, however, the base rate of referrals for initial assessments remained low.

Informal estimates of eligible candidates for AEC referrals suggested that between 5% and 40% of offenders appearing in the District Court on any day would fit the criteria for an initial assessment. (This was based on attendance and nonparticipant observation of court sessions selected at random). An average District Court session might process between 40 and 50 offenders in one morning; it was paradoxical that referrals for AECs remained at a low level (i.e., an average of one per week throughout the study) in a context where 10 eligible candidates might be sentenced in one morning.

Forfar

Establishment of an AEC service in Forfar was developed from an existing court service. A referral system had been established with the Sheriff Courts and AEC services were developed from this template; since 1982, referrals had remained steady at 14 to 18 per year with completion of two or three AECs per year.

Referrals to the Forfar AEC were maintained at an average of one or two per month for the duration of the study.

Comparison of referral rates between Dundee and Forfar indicated some common features: for example, a "seasonal peak" during November/December occurred in both services.

Glasgow

One reason for establishment of AECs in Glasgow was to develop services in a climate where a high rate of referrals would occur. This replication study was based in Glasgow because of a request from the courts for such services and the high number of offenders in the "busiest courts in Europe."

The base-rate referrals for 1987 were, however, similar to the mean monthly referral figures found in Dundee and Forfar.

System Resistance

The low referral rates in Dundee, Forfar, and Glasgow remained a major obstacle to the establishment of controlled evaluation studies in Scotland. While some resistance to these services had been anticipated after the collapse of the 1982 study, difficulties experienced within judicial systems remained intractable.

System resistance to the establishment of AECs, however, was not unique to Scotland; other AECs have failed to flourish despite apparent support for such initiatives within the judicial system (Goodman & Scott, 1982). Other AEC services have been abandoned by the legal system despite initial support and encouragement; one AEC service in northeast England was terminated when the project worker was not reemployed despite available funds to continue the service (Warden, 1986).

Despite recognition of the intrinsic problem of establishment of AECs in any location, the need remained to resolve these problems at local level in Dundee, Forfar, and Glasgow.

A range of specific interventions was attempted in one or more of the three locations, including:

Information Dissemination: Background information about AECs was distributed regularly to a range of sources throughout the research project. These sources included justices, sheriffs, Clerks of Court, solicitors, social workers, and the

Council on Alcohol. These quarterly information bulletins (single sheet of A4) were designed to promote knowledge about the AEC services, to inform users about new developments, and to increase referrals for AECs. They were sent both to individuals and organizations.

Monitoring and Feedback: A commitment was made in all three locations to attend business meetings of the judiciary; in Dundee and Glasgow, quarterly justices meetings were attended to give progress reports, feedback on outcomes, and to provide factual information to specific questions from court officials.

In Dundee and Forfar, contact had been established with individual sheriffs and regular meetings occurred in both locations to monitor progress and provide feedback on outcome.

Direct Appeals: Several attempts were made to increase referrals by direct appeal to specific individuals (e.g., sheriffs; Clerks of Court). These appeals were made by telephone or via personal contact at formal/informal meetings. Such appeals were direct requests for more referrals for eligible AEC candidates.

Who is the Client?

The persistent and intractable difficulties involved in modifying the behavior of referral agents provided a major challenge to successful establishment and implementation of AEC services. Slow referral rates also produced a set of unwanted negative consequences, including difficulties in forming AEC groups, increased rates of attrition because of delays in responding to problems, and devaluing of service because of lack of visible effects.

The low referral rates found in all three locations were consistent with other studies that reported similar problems in recruitment of offender/clients for alcohol education interventions (e.g., Goodman & Scott, 1982; McLoone et al., 1986). This finding also was consistent with previous experiences of attempts to establish AECs in local settings (Robertson & Heather, 1982a).

Several explanations were offered by the justices for nonreferral of more offender/clients. These included:

1. absence of "chronic" drinking problem—clients considered to be not deteriorated enough for an AEC
2. presence of "chronic" drinking problem—clients considered to be too deteriorated for an AEC
3. discrepancy between attitude and behavior—some justices "forgot" to refer clients
4. ineligibility—clients were too old for the AEC (i.e., aged older than 30 years)
5. client refusal—some clients did not want to attend an AEC.

A review of these explanations suggests that (1), (2), and (3) were spurious and were rationalizations of noncooperation by particular justices. Examinations of (4) and (5) suggests that these were legitimate grounds to refuse to refer offender/clients for an AEC interview.

Further consideration of these intractable referral problems produced a revision of the appropriate focus for research enquiry; whereas all initial interventions had been focused on the behavior of teenage and young adult offenders, a change of focus was required to investigate the behavior of referral agents (i.e., justices).

Kilmarnock Courts

Initial contact was made by a senior social worker involved with provision of court services in Kilmarnock; an invitation was made to provide some teaching to a judiciary training session. Further contact with the justices and other court officials produced a wider interest in the establishment of assessment/AEC services to the District and/or Sheriff Courts.

An Experimental Intervention

Implementation of AEC services in Kilmarnock would require prior establishment of sufficient referrals from the District/Sheriff Courts. Previous experience in other settings had raised the question of nonreferral of offender/clients for screening interviews.

An examination of the referral base rates suggested that the District Courts could provide sufficient candidates to establish an AEC; several eligible young offenders had appeared in court during periods of random observation of sentencing procedures. Informal observation of court procedures had raised the question of possible influence of sentencing practices related to the physical presence of alcohol agency staff; some court officials also had observed informally that the presence of alcohol agency staff in court would increase the probability of referral to the agency.

Experimental Hypothesis

The study was based on the hypothesis that it would be possible to modify the sentencing behavior of court officials from simple interventions in the court. Specifically, it was hypothesized that the presence in the court of alcohol agency staff would increase the probability of referral for an AEC assessment.

Design

Two studies were designed to last for several months, using reversal designs. Baseline conditions during the A phase were based on nonattendance at the court by alcohol agency staff.

Thus, although court staff were aware of the possibility of a sentencing option including a recommendation for an AEC assessment, there was no physical presence in the court by agency staff.

The intervention condition during the B phase was based on the physical presence of alcohol agency staff in the district courtroom 2 days per week. The physical presence required the staff only to sit in court and did not specify particular interventions during court proceedings. The staff member was not required to give advice or make representation to the court.

Two studies were implemented during 12 months (Figure 9.1). First, an ABA design was initiated in the Kilmarnock District Court. Second, a BABA design was implemented in the same courts.

Results from Study One indicated an increase in referrals from baseline (A) to intervention (B) conditions. The expected reversal and return to baseline conditions at (A′) did not occur, however, and a further increase in referrals was recorded.

Results of Study Two indicate elevated referral rate during the interventions (B) conditions, followed by a decrease during the return to baseline conditions (A). Reintroduction of the experimental intervention (B′) produced an elevation to the previous referral rate; establishment of return to baseline conditions (A′) produced an initial decrease, followed by a further decrease to zero.

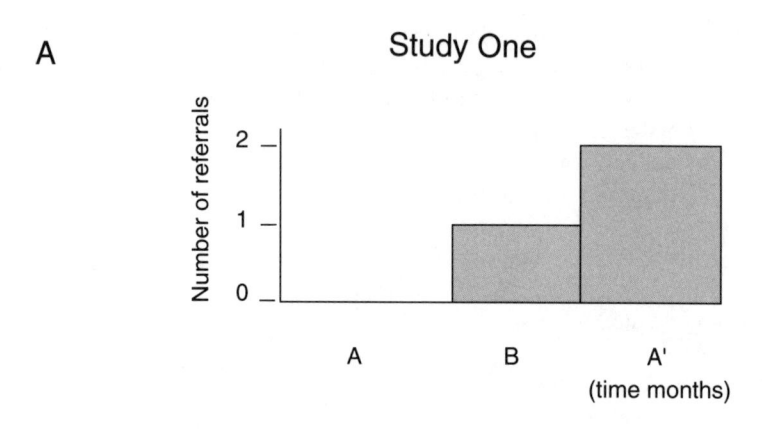

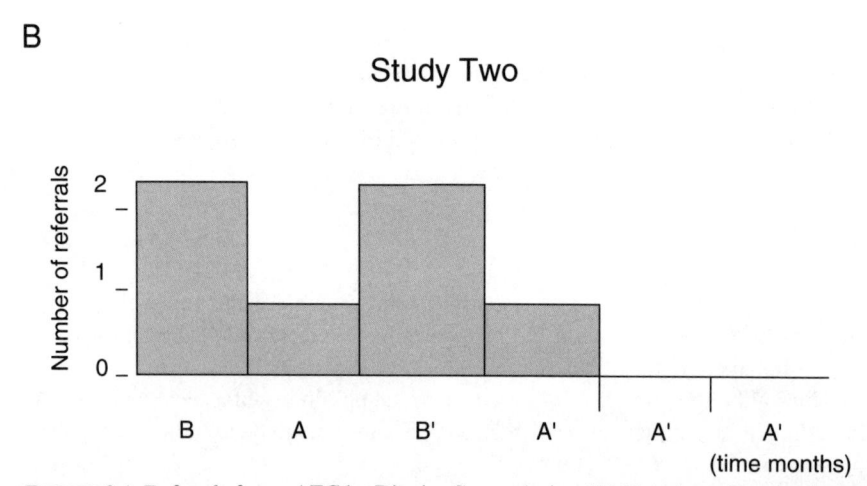

FIGURE 9.1. Referrals for an AEC by District Courts during (A) Non-Attendance and (B) Attendance by Alcohol Agency Staff.

Interpretation

The findings of the two studies are somewhat consistent with the expected effects derived from the experimental hypothesis. Introduction of the experimental intervention was associated with a modest increase in referrals for AEC assessments during that month.

The exception to this finding was during the return to baseline (A') condition in Study One. The observed increase in referrals during that month may have been due to an extraneous confounding factor. Specifically, the increased rate was likely due to a seasonal increase observed in all courts during the winter months.

Discussion

It is possible to exert an impact on the courts via simple interventions. The findings are consistent with the expectation that a modest improvement may be obtained in referral rates from the introduction of a physical presence in the courtroom. These findings have provided some encouragement for interventions within court settings to influence the sentencing behavior of magistrates/justices, which has proved intractable in several previous studies.

Furthermore, this study has provided the "setting conditions" for other similar interventions that might be tested in field experiments (e.g., provision of written information to court officials, examination and amendment of court lists, physical interventions in courts). Other pilot studies have indicated that provision of information about availability of AEC sentencing options in Magistrates Court may increase referral rates (Menary, 1986).

Summary

One implication of this report is that it may be possible to obtain consistent and reliable changes in sentencing behavior of court officials. These findings require replication in other settings to ensure generalizability in time and place.

Informal feedback from other court officials confirms the belief that justices/magistrates may fail to refer offender/clients for alternative educational sentencing options because new learning has not occurred to increase the probability of this behavior. Active interventions may be required in court settings to promote this new learning.

10

Discussion

The aim of this chapter is to integrate the completed studies to achieve a synthesis of the experimental evaluations with young offenders with drinking problems. Data on effectiveness between the studies are compared for similarities, differences and trends.

The analytic techniques used in this evaluation research have all been based on assumptions about the normal distribution of data, equality of subgroup variance, linear associations between variables, and additive effects. Whereas such assumptions are commonplace in evaluation research, in reality data are almost never normally distributed (Kraemer, 1981). The conclusions obtained in such a research context have been limited in their potency and generality.

Results Overview

Dundee Study

Both types of interventions affected offending behavior. The behavioral AEC impacted on weekly drinking levels, whereas in the talk-based AEC the impact of the interventions was insufficient to retard an increase in weekly drinking. Both interventions were associated with a reduction in offenses against people, property, and rules/regulations. Test instruments suggest follow-up improvement in the behavioral AEC group but not the talk-based AEC group on a measure of "alcohol dependence," general health, and attitudes to drinking.

The study reports effectiveness data on comparisons of two types of group-based interventions. While some improvements were noted for talk-based AEC groups, equal or greater differences were observed for behavioral AEC groups. Also, the target-specific contents of behavioral AEC groups were more likely to impact on specific drinking behaviors of offender/clients (e.g., drinking patterns). Clients who completed a behavioral AEC course were more likely to shift their drinking style to a less heavy pattern.

Given the high attrition rates from talk-based AECs and clients' subjective positive ratings for behavioral AECs, however, behavioral AEC provision may be preferable. The additional gains/improvements in drinking behavior from behavioral AEC completion (not found after talk-based AEC completion) may indicate a greater need for this service provision.

Glasgow Study

The very low numbers of offender/clients in the study has precluded firm conclusions. Comparisons between outcome data at follow-up indicated a reduction in weekly volume intake for clients who completed a behavioral AEC compared to clients who had completed a talk-based AEC. In addition, however, an increase was observed in the pretest/post test average scores of weekly drinking by clients who completed a behavioral AEC. This finding (corroborated by the other studies) suggests that clients who have been given alcohol information about "safer" levels of drinking (i.e., 35 units in 1985–1988) may *decrease or increase to that level.*

In addition to differences in drinking behavior, a significant decrease occurred in the pretest/post test offending behavior in the behavioral AEC data. Completion of a behavioral AEC also was associated with reductions in "number of other life problems." Whereas reduction in conviction rates was achieved in the behavioral AEC group, however, there were small increases in self-reported offenses against rules/regulations and persons. Similar, larger effects in the talk-based AEC group may indicate the impact of an extraneous variable (e.g., shift in court sentencing policies).

The very high attrition rates and negative subjective feedback from offender/clients who were referred to talk-based AECs indicated that behavioral AECs may be the intervention of choice in this client population. In addition, there was some evidence of a general deterioration among clients in the talk-based AEC group.

A partial replication of the Dundee study confirms the greater effectiveness as an intervention on offending and drinking behaviors of the behavioral AEC, although interpretations are restricted by limitations of the data.

Perth/Forfar Study

The finding of reductions in several domains (e.g., life problems, self-reported offending behavior) among control group subjects confirms that some improvements in experimental groups may be explained by "time effects" or "reactivity effects." Control groups outcome data confirm that the impact of pretest and follow-up interviews exerted some effects on some offender/client behaviors.

Completion of an information-based AEC, however, was associated with reductions in weekly drinking levels not found in the control group. Provision of information about alcohol and its effects was associated with a reduction in volume intake at follow-up. The information-based AEC, however, did not impact on drinking styles or patterns and did not impact on offending behavior. Moreover, small increases in self-reported offending occurred in the information-based AEC at follow-up, while reductions occurred within the control group. While reductions in control group offending behavior might have been due to regression effects, the information-based AEC did not impact on this domain.

Information-based AECs were associated with reduced weekly volume intake of alcohol at follow-up, but there was no associated reductions in other domains of drinking behavior or in the domain of offending behavior.

Completion of two assessment interviews may produce similar outcome improvements to an information-based AEC.

Noranside Study

Completion of a behavioral AEC by prerelease incarcerated young offenders with drinking problems achieved significant differences at follow-up when compared with a no-intervention control group. Behavioral AEC offender/clients reported reduced weekly volume intake, fewer offenses against rules and regulations, and fewer offenses against persons.

In the control group, which received pretest and follow-up interviews only, there were many increases in alcohol intake at follow-up, including units per week, units per drinking session, and units during "heavy" drinking sessions. In addition, there were increases in "other life problems" and property offenses among the control group, with reductions among the behavioral AEC group. Despite the absence of learning opportunities to acquire skills in (a) "nonoffending," (b) controlled drinking/abstinence via behavioral rehearsal, (c) goal setting, (d) self-monitoring, and (e) feedback, exposure to therapeutic materials may have "set the conditions" for subsequent behavior change. In addition, completion of a behavioral AEC may have promoted positive decision making about reduced drinking and modified offending behavior. In this study, a younger age group (17–21 years) was recruited. This contrasted with the older (17–29 years) range in the noninstitutional studies. Improved outcome from completion of a behavioral AEC may be age related.

These positive results from a more rigorous experimental evaluation favor the further experimental use of behavioral AECs with prerelease young offenders in institutions. The very high demand for such interventions among inmates in such settings, combined with reductions in conviction rates and drinking behaviors at follow-up, have set the conditions for further evaluation studies in similar settings. Subsequent studies should consider costs and benefits of no-intervention control groups, given the apparent benefits of behavioral AEC interventions.

Overview

All studies have limitations of statistical conclusion validity (assumed covariation between AECs and drinking/offending behaviors), internal validity (assumed causal relationship between AECs and behavior), construct validity (generalizability of relationships to and across populations of persons, settings, and times), and reporting adequacy (achievement of minimal requirements of precision and replicability). Future studies should review efforts to monitor interventions to improve reporting adequacy (Shapiro & Shapiro, 1983).

Dundee Long-Term Follow-Up (1981 Study)

Despite the limitations of uncontrolled evaluative studies, the long-term follow-up data of the original 1981 cohort suggest some tentative conclusions:

1. conviction rates were reduced to near zero within 2 years of AEC completion
2. all offenders reported 2 or more offense-free years in the 5 years after AEC completion
3. most offenders reported some positive benefits of an AEC at follow-up and attributed change to the course
4. most offenders reported lower volume intake alcohol levels at follow-up (≥ 40 units)
5. all offenders were aged 24 or older at follow-up.

Kilmarnock Study

Results from a preliminary study suggest that simple interventions in public courts may help resolve chronic and persistent problems of nonreferral to AECs.

Implementation of a short-term intervention (i.e., physical presence of an alcohol specialist in the court 2 days per week for 1 month) was associated with a small increase in referral rates. Withdrawal of the experimental condition was associated with a reduction in the referral rate; this effect was achieved in a BABA reversal study.

Although the experimental effect was modest, the results of this study suggest that similar court-based interventions may exert an impact on the behavior of court officials. Sentencing practices in judicial environments have been notoriously difficult to influence and highly resistant to change attempts. These results may set the conditions for subsequent evaluation studies of similar court-based interventions.

Clients

In all studies, two dependent variables were measured: drinking behavior and offending behavior. Although there were some indirect methods of validation (i.e., via corroborative reports from collateral interviews), most measures were based on self-report data. One study reported multisource data to corroborate self-reported offending data.

The reliability and validity of self-report data has been the subject of much debate (e.g., Midanik, 1982; Watson et al., 1984). Whereas problem drinkers may create special challenges for monitoring, outcome measures, and evaluation, the use of self-reports has been well established in the field of behavior therapy/behavior modification (e.g., Hersen, 1978). Conclusions from this debate have focused on the need to include multisource data collection to provide corroborative or collateral information about clients' drinking levels. Such measures have been used in some studies at the alcohol/offending interface (e.g., Myers, 1983). On balance, the reliability of self-reports of drinking behavior of offender/clients may be subject to distortions of over reporting *and* under reporting: these biases may covary with stages of change.

The quality of offending behavior data requires scrutiny. In particular, when "crime rates" are used as a dependent variable, this always involves imperfect measurement: conviction rate decreases should be substantial before they can be attributed to factors other than chance variation (Zimring, 1976). As evaluations of correctional interventions have relied on outcome measures associated with repenetration of the criminal justice system (i.e., reconviction rates), the use of such measures ideally should be based on long-term follow-ups of 36 months (Hudson, 1977).

In addition, change attempts from social programs in the criminal justice field have been limited in potency from relatively weak and diluted interventions. Unrealistic expectations have been generated about possible effects from puny and time-limited interventions (Hudson, 1977).

Other limitations on improvement on dependent variables (drinking/offending behaviors) may have been due to inadequate consideration for generalization across time, places, and persons. Such generalization was limited to "train and hope" strategies rather than based on sequential modification, natural maintaining contingencies, training sufficient exemplars, or loose training (Stokes & Baer, 1977).

In addition, the studies may have been subject to type one errors where functional significance has been rejected when it should have been accepted. Type two errors will have been less likely to occur: it is unlikely that functional relationships will have been accepted when they should have been rejected.

The presence of type one errors would have indicated a misattribution of effects obtained from random effects to an experimental effect that was not present. In this situation, the inaccurate affirmation of functional significance between the experimental intervention and observed differences in dependent variables would be due to mistaken beliefs about the source and cause of changes obtained. Specifically, such differences often may be best explained by changes in life events.

Such life events were documented during baseline and follow-up interventions with the young offenders. The MSI was designed to include specific questions about variables commonly associated with change in life events in drinking populations (Marlatt & Miller, 1984). Such variables included housing status, family status, marital status, employment, and education. These qualitative variables might have been expected to influence outcome at follow-up.

With few exceptions, however, these variables were not associated with changes in dependent variables in experimental or control groups. None of these measures was a predictor variable for outcome in the analysis between groups. There were several offenders who completed behavioral AECs who also made changes in their housing, employment, or educational status; these individuals, however, were rare. On balance, life events recorded in self-report interviews were not found to co-vary with changes in dependent variables. While other intervening variables (e.g., help seeking) may have exerted effects on the behavior or experiences of the client population, these were not examined in this study.

Outcome

Offender/clients with alcohol problems have been notoriously resistant to change attempts, both in institutions and in local neighborhood settings (Blackburn, 1980; Stumphauzer, 1979, 1986). Many practitioners have adopted the "nothing works" philosophy, which may have contributed to the negative climate and "setting conditions" for work with offenders.

Results from these experimental studies have suggested that AECs may have a positive impact on some drinking behaviors. In particular, information-based, talk-based, and behavioral AECs all affect weekly alcohol intake. Behavioral AECs, however, exert an additional impact on offending behavior that does not occur with other AEC intervention types. This impact of behavioral AECs was greatest in the population of prerelease incarcerated young offenders: clients in noninstitutional settings also improved at follow-up when compared with talk-based AECs.

The effectiveness of information-based AECs on offender/client outcomes at follow-up was minimal, given the relative costs and benefits. Although the information-based AEC impacted on weekly drinking limits, there was no improvement of conviction rates at follow-up when compared with a no-intervention control group.

These data raise the question about the validity of continued information-based AEC service provision. Ninety percent of United Kingdom services are information-based AECs (Gamba et al., 1989). There have been no data on effectiveness based on controlled evaluations, however. Although some recent claims have been made for effectiveness of information-based counselling/AECs (Collins & Tate, 1988; Menary, 1988), these have been based on uncontrolled studies using post hoc analysis. Such studies may have made a contribution toward the eventual implementation of controlled evaluation studies on effectiveness; they are of limited value, however, when compared with outcome data from empirical studies.

Predictor Variables

Identification of predictor variables from limited data has provided a challenge for results interpretation. Problems of methodology and implementation have restricted such identification from a relatively small sample size. Despite these limitations, however, some variables may predict improved client outcome from completion of an AEC. These include age, AEC type, problem chronicity, drinking problems, and attrition.

AGE

These studies suggest that younger offender/clients (17–21 years) from the total sample population (17–29 years) are more likely to improve on offending/behaviors. (This is based in part on subjective observations of older offenders, who often expressed very negative feedback about AECs and also were often highly resistant to change during AECs.) Younger clients (17–21 years) were most likely to attend for an MSI assessment at first request from the court: this increased probability of attendance was enhanced if they were also requested to telephone to confirm their willingness to attend for interview on the same day of their court appearance. This is consistent with improvements obtained among offender/clients in the same age range in the Noranside study.

ALCOHOL EDUCATION COURSE TYPE

Clients referred to a behavioral AEC were more likely to complete the intervention than clients referred for either a talk-based AEC or an information-based AEC. Talk-based AECs produced highest attrition rates. In addition talk-based AECs may be contraindicated in offender/clients who require a high degree of structure in their programming; given free choice, offender/clients with alcohol-related problems will choose an action-based behavioral AEC "package" rather than a discursive talk-based AEC.

PROBLEM CHRONICITY

Offending/drinking problem chronicity did not seem to predict outcome following an AEC, as might have been expected. Although there was limited evidence for improved response among clients with three or fewer offenses, it was not a reliable predictor of outcome.

DRINKING PATTERNS

In three studies, a shift to a "less heavy drinking pattern" was associated with a reduction in conviction rates. A predictor of subsequent offending at longer term follow-up (i.e., 24 months, 36 months, 48 months) may relate to this prior achievement of a less heavy drinking pattern.

The subsequent achievement of this heavy drinking pattern (e.g., "binge" drinking to "weekly" drinking) may reduce the probability of episodic heavy drinking. Given the increased probability of offending behavior during periods of extreme intoxication, this achievement of less heavy drinking patterns may exert a prophylactic effect on subsequent offending behavior.

ATTRITION

In all studies, attrition diminished the effective sample size and hence the power and sensitivity of statistical techniques. Attrition may not have been random among comparison groups or across client variables to provide experimental control. This may have produced inaccurate assessment of the relationships between AECs and drinking/offending behaviors.

Preinclusion attrition occurred in all studies, which reduced sample representativeness of the wider client population and may have increased the probability of misattribution of an independent variable/dependent variable relationship. Such a relationship may be explained by attrition-related client variables. Equally, differences in postinclusion attrition rates suggest that causes of attrition will be different. Even when "attrition fractions" may be similar across groups, comparability of groups may have been lost, as similar rates do not imply similar causation. The most conservative method to deal with attrition may be to eliminate from analysis any cases missing independent variable data and use only cases not missing data on a dependent variable in any analysis involving the dependent variable (Howard et al., 1986). While subsequent tests of differences between "completers" and "attritors" in all studies revealed few statistically significant differences, client attrition in future AEC evaluations will require further investigation. Among an offender/client population, the pretense of control over attrition is inappropriate.

Very high attrition rates occurred for talk-based AECs in both studies; this was based partly on unfavorable views of offender/clients who had expected a high degree of structure, direction, and problem-specific contents. Many clients expressed negative statements about talk-based AECs; in contrast, most clients who completed a behavioral AEC made positive statements about the course. This may have been due to differences in the "set" with which clients arrived for intervention (e.g., Kazdin, 1978). In particular, different rates of attrition may have been caused by differences in "perceived credibility" by clients and of intervention and control conditions (Shapiro & Shapiro, 1983). Future studies should aim to eliminate (or at least reduce) differential client expectations of benefit as the source of outcome differences (i.e., nonspecific effects).

On three occasions, attrition from talk-based AECs was sufficient to prevent continuation, which produced abandonment of the course (remaining clients were offered 1:1 alcohol counseling outwith the study). Attrition on behavioral AECs rarely exceeded one client per course: the high degree of contracting and group cohesion achieved in behavioral AECs usually reduced the probability to zero of client dropout after completion of session one. Attrition levels on information-based AECs exceeded levels on behavioral AECs. In the Forfar study, on average, two clients dropped out of information-based AECs during their progress: this may have been due to the absence of a specific contract to maintain attendance during the course. Attrition rates from other information-based AECs in the national provision of services has remained unknown. There is some evidence, however, that failure to maintain offender/clients in AECs may be related to type of course (Warden, 1986).

Intervention-correlated self-selection is not uncommon in such studies; it will be most likely to occur when participants perceive some kind of cost in receiving their assigned intervention and when interventions differ in attractiveness (Cook, Cook & Mark, 1977). In addition, intervention-correlated attrition may occur when program participants differentially drop out of an evaluation before it is completed. Differential rates of attrition across interventions was observed; attrition rates were higher for talk-based AECs than for behavioral AECs (28% and 9% in the Dundee study). This phenomenon is common in longitudinal research, where subjects may perceive different costs or gains associated with different interventions.

Intervention-correlated attrition can produce major threats to internal validity. Several methods exist, however, to detect the presence of differential attrition: tests for differences in percentages of lost units across groups, and testing for pretreatment means that are different across treatment groups, after individuals who did not provide post test data have been deleted. Alternatively, persons who agree to stay in the interventions, regardless of which intervention they might be assigned by chance, can be randomly assigned to interventions (Cook et. al., 1977). An optimum strategy to prevent selection bias that might produce spurious positive results is to produce two sets of statistical data, one time including people who did not receive the assigned intervention and another time omitting them. Lack of comparability indicates caution in drawing conclusions.

Follow-Ups

Achievement of follow-up information from young offenders with alcohol problems has been notoriously difficult because of client characteristics such as moves in residence, source data unreliability, subsequent incarceration, geographical mobility, records inadequacy, client resistance to reinterview, and subsequent reconviction and readmission to legal systems. In addition, there have been some recent challenges to the necessity of follow-up assessment in outcome research (Nicholson & Berman, 1983). Potential benefits of follow-up evaluations should be balanced against costs. Research in addictive behaviors may, however, result in a greater need for follow-up evaluation (McFall, 1978; Nathan & Lansky, 1978).

In all studies, at least 60% of all clients were reinterviewed at follow-up (range 60–100%). Higher percentages of completed follow-ups would have been preferable to reduce the probability of unrepresentative sampling from the cohort. The present studies may be limited in generalizability, however, because of nonrepresentative sampling during follow-up (e.g., reliance on written/telephone contact to arrange follow-up appointment). They are, however, consistent with other, similar studies in the field that have reported 60% follow-up rates across conditions (e.g., Spence, 1979).

The payment of five pounds to all interviewees at follow-up, while a potential confounding variable, was essential for interviewee compliance. Although payment for a completed interview added another variable, it was a prerequisite for subsequent interviews, in the absence of consequences of a court tariff. Nonetheless, payment for participation may have introduced another source of variability (Nicholson & Berman, 1983).

Medium-term follow-up data (i.e., 9–15 months) was achieved in all studies. This is consonant with data obtained from meta-analysis studies of outcome research (i.e., only 6% of studies obtained data 4 or more months after the end of the intervention) (Shapiro & Shapiro, 1983). It is also consonant with mean follow-up periods obtained in other outcome studies (i.e., 8 months) (Nicholson & Berman, 1983). Subsequent controlled evaluations should include short-term (3-month) and long-term (24- or 36 month) data. Inclusion of 3-month data is based on the observation that outcome data at this time may predict subsequent progress in the population of drinking offenders. Inclusion of 24-month data would be required to confirm durability of medium-term gains in drinking/offending behaviors. Also, with some evidence from a 30-year follow-up that interventions with offenders *increased* subsequent offending behavior (McCord, 1978), a major commitment is required to adopt a long-term perspective on such evaluations.

All follow-ups were completed by interviewers "blind" to the experimental hypothesis. Before the interviews, interviewers were requested to tell clients:

> Do not tell me whether or not you have completed an alcohol education course. We can discuss this after the interview has been completed.

Despite this instruction to interviewees, however, the demand characteristics of the interview situation may have rewarded subjects for "faking well" for the interviewer. Despite the absence of an impending court appearance (and subsequent sentencing tariff), the responses of subjects may have been affected by systematic bias to present themselves in a favorable light (Rosenthal, 1966). Equally, however, this effect of "faking well" may have been counterbalanced by an opposite effect to over-report "negative" information (e.g., offending behavior, heavy drinking). Such over-reporting may be endemic in young offender/drinker populations.

In addition, the study may have been flawed by the absence of a debriefing questionnaire. Future studies would be much improved with the introduction of such a questionnaire to determine whether offender/clients in the cohort knew each other. These data would be used to examine possible effects on "subject contamination" via inadvertent or deliberate transmission between clients of the experimental hypothesis (Orne, 1962). In the clinical population of offender/clients it is probable that some subjects knew others in the cohort. Such possible "contamination effects" would be largest in the rural population centres (i.e., Perth and Forfar) and less likely in larger cities (i.e., Dundee and Glasgow). Future research should include such debriefing measures.

Sex Differences

During the establishment of all noninstitutional AEC services, referrals were requested for young offender/clients aged between 17 to 29 years, regardless of sex. Moreover, in the Dundee and Glasgow studies active strategies were used to recruit female offender/clients into the study.

Despite these attempts, however, no referrals were received in Glasgow for female offender/clients. In Dundee, three referrals were received in 24 months of service provision.

Nonparticipant observation in District Courts indicated a potential population of offender/clients eligible for an AEC. Specifically, female offender/clients formed up to 15% of eligible clients during most District Court sessions. Referral of such clients for MSI assessment, however, was extremely rare despite active soliciting for referrals for female offenders.

A recent review of national AEC services indicated that 76% of United Kingdom agencies provide courses for males and females; 9/55 (16%) agencies provided female-only AECs (Gamba et al., 1989). The resistance to refer female offenders in these Scottish studies suggests a bias within legal systems.

This bias may be related to discrimination and selective processing at other junctures in the criminal justice system: police behaviors, arrest behavior, and sentencing procedures may all affect client outcomes within the system (Iglehart & Stein, 1985). Institutionalized sexism via discriminatory practices may account for the low rate of female referrals into AEC studies. The perception of female offending behavior as a "psychiatric" (sic) not social/interpersonal problem (McLaughlin, 1985) may have reduced the probability of referral to these social interventions. Also, a rehabilitation program for female offender/clients based on male models of offending/drinking behaviors may be inadequate and inappropriate to the problem (Crawshaw, 1990; Fodor, 1972).

On balance, the effectiveness of AECs with female offender/clients has remained unevaluated. No controlled studies have been attempted; most AEC service provision has been based on a heterosocial mix of clients. Evaluation of single-sex male AECs and female AECs remains an evaluation priority.

Clinical/Statistical/Functional Significance

Although some social programs may achieve statistical significance levels, the practical implications may be trivial. Thus, it is possible almost to guarantee statistical significance (regardless of the real size of intervention effects) from very large sample sizes (Berk & Brewer, 1977). The present studies reported statistical significance levels but a similar emphasis was aimed at investigation of clinical significance.

As yet, there is no standard procedure or measurement strategy to assess clinical significance (Kazdin, 1986). Other measures in addition to outcome measures may require consideration. Attrition rates and client evaluations of interventions may reflect important practical differences between AECs that are otherwise similar in outcome. Themes such as costs, efficiency, risk and acceptability merit further investigation. Several studies produced results that, although not achieving statistical significance, achieved clinical significance.

Specifically, behavioral AECs did not always achieve significant improvement on all variables but the trend of such interventions was usually positive. The overall trends suggested a modest but positive impact of behavioral AECs on drinking and offending behaviors and in other life domains. At least these interventions inoculated offender/clients against some of the deteriorations observed among control group clients.

The "natural course" of drinking/offending patterns among control group clients suggested that, while pretest/post-test interviews impacted on some client behaviors, mean number of units per week (31.7; 31.6) and mean number of units in "heavy drinking week" (94.6; 98.2) remained constant between baseline and a 16-month follow-up. Despite reductions in other domains, many alcohol-related offending behaviors remained unmodified (or were exacerbated) from random effects over time.

Statistically significant results in several domains were achieved in the institutional (Noranside) study. This study produced the clearest indication of intervention effectiveness, based on a controlled evaluation with a more rigorous methodology and implementation. In other studies, functional significance (i.e., reduction/amelioration of offending and drinking behaviors) was observed on several variables. In addition, behavioral AECs may have exerted a preventative, prophylactic effect in other life domains.

In addition to these differences of statistical and functional significance, other differences of clinical significance were observed among some offender/clients at follow-up. For some clients the cultural meaning of their drinking behavior had changed. In particular, at the initial MSI many clients reported highly maladaptive drinking patterns when asked about their "attitudes to alcohol" and "reasons for drinking"; in addition, many offenders used alcohol as an instrumental activity prior to other offending behaviors.

While statistical analysis did not produce significant differences between (or within) groups on "attitudes to alcohol" or "reasons for drinking" at follow-up, many clients' drinking patterns suggested alterations in their cultural use of alcohol. Self-reports from some clients corroborated this impression of an alteration in the meaning attached to drinking alcohol. Some clients, for example, stated that they no longer drank alcohol to achieve extremes of intoxication; "drinking to oblivion" had been rejected by some offender/clients during their AEC.

Similarly, the *meaning* of "committing offenses" and "staying out of trouble" seemed to have been reversed for some clients. Whereas many offender/clients attached a positive value to committing offenses at baseline interviews, many clients who completed behavioral AECs reported a subsequent reversal of values (i.e., negative toward committing offenses and positive toward moderate/controlled drinking). The cultural meaning of offending/drinking behaviors among a client population who may use both activities for extensive avoidance/escape patterns merits further empirical investigation.

Test Instruments

Administration of the GHQ produced reliable reductions between baseline and follow-up measures in all studies: follow-up scores always were less than scores at baseline. This effect, however, may be explained by statistical regression, instrumentation insensitivity, or reactive assessment (or a combination of these effects). As a reliable barometer of change among young offender/clients with drinking problems, however, the GHQ is unpromising.

Attitudes to Drinking Questionnaire

As a measure of clinical change, the Attitudes to Drinking Questionnaire may offer a more sensitive instrument that can detect shifts in drinking patterns via attitude measures. Despite the limitations of attitude measurement (Midanik, 1982), this may offer a complementary framework to behavioral self-report measures.

MAST

Interpretation of MAST scores indicated that all AEC interventions reduced average scores to lower levels; this finding was confounded by the observation that similar reductions were obtained in the control population. As a reliable measure of behavioral change among young offenders, the MAST does not provide a sensitive instrument for subsequent use.

SADQ

The SADQ was used as a screening instrument to detect the presence of "alcohol dependence." In practice, most offender/clients did not score above the cut off on pretest or follow-up scores. Several offender/clients who had recorded high SADQ scores were not included in group AECs but were offered one to one counseling. Several other clients who had recorded high pretest SADQ scores did not attend AECs because of admissions into other services (e.g., psychiatric/general hospitals). Use of SADQ as a research/diagnostic tool remains promising (Hodgson et al., 1978; Stockwell, Hodgson, Edwards, Taylor, & Rankin, 1979; Stockwell, Murphy, & Hodgson, 1983).

On balance, some test instruments included may have been inappropriate to the needs of young offenders. In particular, some of the instruments may have been subject to reactive assessment. With reference to outcome measures, such instruments varied from slightly to highly reactive (Shapiro & Shapiro, 1983). Inclusion of more client-specific and problem-specific materials remains a high priority for subsequent controlled evaluations.

Subsequent evaluation research could aim to include specific assessment techniques superimposed on a standard assessment battery of behavior change. Additionally, such research might include process measures as a partial test of the model underlying different AECs. Further consideration is required of the interval between completion of intervention and administration of test instruments at follow-up; changes on different types of measures (and measures of different constructs) may vary with the duration of this interval (Rachman & Hodgson, 1974).

Staff/Workers

In England and Wales, 78% of AECs are provided by probation officers/social workers (Gamba et al., 1989). In Scotland, involvement of social workers in similar service provision had been minimal despite some local exceptions (Baldwin, Ford, & Heather, 1987; Baldwin, Ford, Heather, & Braggins, 1987). Nonetheless, subsequent involvement of social workers in future AEC services may represent a cost-effective use of resources. Involvement by social services staff in group-based interventions should remain a high priority in a system constrained by limited resources.

One contraindication to involvement of social workers/probation officers in AECs remains the conflict of interest produced from the disclosure of "actionable" material by offender/clients. More specifically, AEC members may be constrained in disclosure of information about their offending behaviors in a context where AEC tutors who are their social workers/probation officers have a wider responsibility to act on this disclosed material (McGuire & Priestley, 1985).

This conflict of interest may be sufficient to prevent the involvement of some probation officers/social workers who should not run AECs. Other solutions are possible, however. For example, social work staff not involved as case workers for AEC members may run AECs without this conflict of interest and with a clear mandate not to disclose material from sessions. Social work staff should not work with AEC clients with whom they are also case workers.

Council on Alcohol Workers

Local Council on Alcohol workers were involved in service design and implementation of evaluation studies in Dundee, Perth, and Glasgow. Nonstatutory counselors were involved as co-counselors on AECs in all three settings and also completed MSI interviews. Some counselors also completed follow-up interviews. Counselor participation in interviews and AECs was completed to criterion. Involvement of nonstatutory Councils on Alcohol in such service provision has been recommended as a national strategy to implement a comprehensive local response to deficits in existing court services (Tether & Robinson, 1986). As independent agencies with a specific remit to address the problems of "secondary prevention," several Councils on Alcohol have been involved in the provision of AECs.

Many of the Council on Alcohol staff involved in the alcohol/offending project did not require extensive teaching or training; most staff achieved criterion in the MSI within 5 hours and most were able to co-tutor an AEC after 2 completed courses. The involvement of such nonstatutory workers in AECs may be highly desirable as a cost-effective form of service provision. In addition, offender/clients often achieved a ready identification with such counselors, who were more free from professional barriers. In keeping with social research guidelines (Reiken & Boruch, 1974), many counselors were able to "speak the same language" as the offender/clients, often from a similar cultural matrix. It did, however, introduce another source of variability into the evaluation research: meta-analysis of control/intervention studies has revealed that therapists/counselors averaged 3 years' experience. The use of untrained counselors with heterogeneous backgrounds and limited skills training may have increased variability in these studies (Shapiro & Shapiro, 1983). The impact of therapists/counselors in outcome research requires further investigation.

Involvement of local Council on Alcohol staff will require consideration of payment for provision of court reports. Whereas payment for other forms of court reports (i.e., psychiatric report) is not unusual, most United Kingdom Councils on

Alcohol have not charged for provision of similar forensic services. Payment for AEC assessment reports will require local Councils on Alcohol to guarantee a minimum standard to document drinking behaviors. Future provision of AEC services by a local Council on Alcohol is consistent with the involvement of special needs services (i.e., secondary drug education) in noninstitutional settings (Tether & Robinson, 1986). Such involvement should be contingent on in-service training of agency staff to achieve criterion performance. This involvement should be complementary to, and not a substitute for, statutory provision by social services.

Teaching/Training

Teaching and training of social services/nonstatutory alcohol agency staff has been a challenge for accomplishment to the alcohol/offending services. Specifically, it has been difficult to guarantee consistency of AECs beyond three initial courses. The original model was based on withdrawal from teaching/training after three AECs in any single location. Despite attempts to maintain standard delivery and uniformity of presentation in different locations, the very process of generalization of the AEC into new settings produced "drift" from the original model. The implementation process of AEC provision produced dilution of the contents, and probable distortions, due to differences in program interpretations by different staff/workers. Such factors may have exerted limitations on the generalizability of the effects obtained (Kazdin, 1978).

In addition, despite some preselection of AEC counselors to exclude persons with rigid, inflexible, or concrete views, each counselor will have adapted the original model according to their own interpretations. Initial precautions to maintain quality and consistency via semistructured materials for behavioral AECs produced only limited success. "Drift" on talk-based AECs (that did not contain fixed session contents) was highly likely to exceed margins of "drift" observed in behavioral AECs. The execution of the interventions might have been improved by the specification of counselors training by length of experience rather than by proficiency of skills (Kazdin, 1986).

Resolution of program drift was viewed as a joint problem for teaching/training and program contents specification. Whereas standardization of talk-based AECs was limited to structural guidelines (e.g., counseling styles), behavioral AECs were more amenable to standardization via "manualization." The aim of behavioral AEC standardization produced the impetus for development of the Ending Offending Training Pack.

Ending Offending

The Ending Offending packs were developed as first attempts at standardization of a behavioral AEC in non-institutional (Baldwin et al., 1988) and institutional (Baldwin et al., 1989) settings. They were based on effectiveness evaluations of AECs in the Scottish alcohol/offending evaluation project. In addition to standardization of program contents via specified use of videos, acetate slides, and behavioral methods (e.g., drink diaries), the pack also included innovative materials specifically developed for the population of young offender/clients (e.g., self-recording cards). Standardization of the training materials was assisted by two manuals that specified the form and content of behavioral AECs.

The Ending Offending training packs are the first standardization initiatives which may set the conditions for subsequent evaluation attempts. The national pattern of AEC service provision in the United Kingdom has been based on the haphazard development of services without a formal or logical structure (Gamba et al., 1989). Standardization of training materials into an agreed format may be the impetus for subsequent adoption and testing in local settings.

Systems

The original research design was based on a series of independent variable/dependent variable studies of AECs on drinking/offending behaviors. Thus, the original focus of these studies was on offender/client behaviors.

District Courts

Chronic implementation problems, however, required a refocus on the courts. In particular, the sentencing behavior of District Court officials was a major barrier to establishment of AEC services in Dundee and Glasgow. Sheriff Court officials, in contrast, maintained high base rates of referrals in Dundee and Perth. (In Dundee, referrals from the Sheriff Court represented 45% of the total; in Perth, two Sheriffs referred 368 clients in 18 months.) In the District Courts, however, referral base rates continued at low frequency despite several modification attempts.

Several rival explanations (or a combination thereof) may account for this phenomenon. These include (a) pressure to give custodial sentences, (b) inconsistency of the same court officials at different times, (c) inconsistency of different court officials at different times, (d) "public opinion" about appropriate sentencing, (e) conflicts of interest for court officials, (f) reelection criteria for Justices/Magistrates, (g) knowledge of sentencing procedures and legal tariffs, (h) consequences for an offender for completion of an AEC, (i) consequences of noncompletion of an AEC, (j) climate for referrals to "controlled drinking" programs, and (k) establishment of "experimental" programs.

Pressure to give custodial sentences in District Courts was an extraneous variable throughout the study. Although this variable may have been subject to fluctuations from the external judiciary system, the "ecological climate" was a known factor: the evaluation research studies were completed in the context of a national administration (and subsequent legislation) committed to "law and order" policies. One effect of these policies in the local context may have been to reduce the probabilities of use of noncustodial sentencing options by the judiciary. In this climate, effectiveness evaluations of noncustodial sentencing options such as AECs may be contextually difficult. Some support for this conclusion is based on observations of other attempts to encourage Scottish courts to adopt other policies of noncustodial sentencing such as diversion schemes (Erikson, 1984).

Inconsistency of justices' sentencing behavior produced a major obstacle to implementation of AEC evaluations throughout the studies. It remained an intractable problem behavior not always amenable to interventions based on simple environmental manipulations or instructional changes. In particular, it was difficult to ensure continuity of sentencing procedures between different justices; an offender/client who appeared before one justice (who favored an AEC disposal) might have this decision reversed when appearing before a different justice. As AEC completion required a minimum of three court appearances for each offender (initial appearance, MSI report, AEC report), this might involve contact with three different justices, with a range of views about problem drinking and its optimum solutions.

In practice, an offender/client might be recommended for an AEC by a justice committed to alternative sentencing policies and subsequently achieve much reform of offending/drinking behaviors. The offender might subsequently appear before a different justice who was committed to an "abstinence model" of alcohol, and also adhere to a policy of custodial sentencing or heavy fining (or both). Thus, while an offender may have modified his/her drinking and/or offending from his/her own efforts during 6 months' reform, this may have been contiguous with a heavy penalty from the subsequent deferred sentence court appearance.

Although there was no explicit relationship between AEC completion and subsequent court sentencing procedures, there was an implicit expectation that court officials might be favorable to genuine reform attempts by young offenders. This contingency between outcome, following AEC completion and inconsistent court sentencing, may have affected the perception of the intervention among users in the main study. In particular, the study may have been subject to contamination effects by clients who had completed an AEC.

The link between "public opinion" and the sentencing policies of District Courts has not been clarified and may not be a linear relationship. In particular, the judiciary may be reactive—not proactive—in their relations with members of the public. In a context where "ordinary members of the public" see themselves at risk from use of noncustodial "soft option" alternatives, this may exert strong effects on justices to adhere to more punitive options. In the context of a conflict of interest for individual justices (e.g., a "law and order" climate during a time of reelection to public office) probabilities dictate that "tried and tested" custodial methods may be best despite lack of data on effectiveness and some data on ineffectiveness (Pratt, 1985).

Limitations of knowledge about sentencing procedures and legal tariffs also may have been a barrier to successful implementation of AEC services. Informal observations of courts in progress and discussions with court officials suggested that many justices relied on Clerks of Court for advice and guidance in practical situations. Resolution of these deficits would be a challenge for the subsequent in-service training of justices.

Recruitment for "controlled drinking" programs has been notoriously difficult in the United Kingdom and United States (Heather, 1986a; Miller, 1983b). In particular, several formal intervention programs based on experimental evaluations of effectiveness have been discontinued, because of chronic and intractable difficulties with client recruitment; some programs have collapsed after 7 years of continuous recruitment problems (Miller, 1983b). This may be related to public perceptions of "controlled drinking" programs and associated problems with implementation of experiments viewed as negative by local neighborhood leaders and dignitaries (Rieken & Boruch, 1974).

Despite the wider range of interventions available to clients (i.e., abstinence programs and controlled drinking programs), the AEC evaluation studies were perceived by service users (e.g., justices) and clients as a controlled drinking program). This may have been due to the rigid, inflexible way in which intervention programs are perceived (as "either/or" options) as well as to perceptions of the specific study. By definition, interventions that are not perceived as "abstinence programs" may be given "controlled drinking" labels. Thus, despite repeated attempts to educate and inform justices via training sessions, information bulletins, and informal contacts, the overall perception of the AEC may have been based on a "soft option," educational (i.e., nonpunitive) alternative to "real" sentencing options.

These perceptions are consonant with previous research projects with offender/clients that have encountered a range of system resistances, including police objections to courts "mollycoddling" offenders, official resistance to investment of funds in programs without guaranteed outcomes, and project initiation during a "law and order" climate (e.g., Davidson & Robinson, 1975). Similarly, successful promotion of alternative sentencing programs for noncustodial options may require more demonstrations of cost-effectiveness savings.

This internal system resistance to refer young offender/clients to AECs has occurred elsewhere in other national settings (e.g., Stevens, 1986) with subsequent collapse of some AECs (e.g., Warden, 1986). These AECs have been established by social workers/probation officers within the service via changes of the internal structure of existing systems. Such workers have set up new service systems or modified existing services to implement AEC provision. Such initiatives have relied on other components of the service system (e.g., judiciary) to support these services directly via referrals.

Other probation workers have adopted a more assertive strategy, by advising the system directly about appropriate forms of service provision (e.g., Menary, 1986). In particular, such workers have attempted to stimulate high base rates of referrals of clients to AECs via active canvassing of the judiciary. Specific methods have been used to bring the AEC sentencing option to the attention of magistrates by increasing the probabilities of consideration of this option. The use of explanatory/advisory leaflets for magistrates, which include the specific phrasing of disposal (i.e., disposal "shall attend, in a sober condition, eight consecutive weekly sessions of an alcohol education group, as directed by the probation officer"), has achieved some success. High base rates have been reported in preliminary studies, where more than 150 clients have been recruited for AECs in 6 months (Menary, 1988).

Although within-system modifications by social workers/probation officers may produce higher base-rates of referrals, a potential conflict of interest may occur. Staff who have high investments in establishment and maintenance of AEC services may over-invest in development at the expense of service evaluation. (Recent claims for 70% "success" for unevaluated AECs have provided one example of this trend). Independent service evaluations are required to ensure objectivity without conflict of interest.

Long-term modifications of practices of justices and magistrates may require extensive interventions to produce shifts in sentencing behavior. Although there is some evidence for modest shifts in referral behavior following simple environmental manipulations in courts (Baldwin & Thomson, 1991), more extensive alterations may require higher level modifications (e.g., legislative changes).

Sheriff Courts

Throughout all studies in Dundee, Forfar, and Perth, the Sheriff Courts provided a consistent and reliable source of referrals for AECs. Despite variations between courts in different locations, all courts regularly referred offender/clients for initial interviews. Base rate referrals in Perth always exceeded referral rates in other courts: the lack of consequences for courts (or court officials) for referral to a no-intervention control group increased the probability of such a recommendation by the sheriffs. This observation is confirmed by the eventual introduction of AECs to Perth in Spring 1988; after completion of the control group, the base rate for referrals decreased from between 10 and 30 per week to between 3 and 7 per week. Nonetheless, the prior establishment of referral procedures to a control group may have "primed" the court system to identify relatively high numbers of potential candidates. This may be an effective strategy for subsequent change attempts in District Courts.

Sheriff Courts may have achieved more consistency in referral/disposal behaviors because of the few people involved. In Dundee and Forfar, one sheriff was responsible for all referrals, and two sheriffs in Perth. None of the problems of AEC services based in the District Court occurred in Sheriff Courts (e.g., low referral rates, inappropriate referral of ineligible clients, idiosyncratic/inconsistent sentencing procedures). In contrast, sheriffs were highly consistent in their sentencing behaviors and worked closely to the identified criteria.

Therefore, despite pressure to give custodial sentences or heavy fines to offenders with relatively more "serious" offense behaviors (e.g., offenses against persons), sheriffs still used AEC sentencing options as an alternative disposal to incarcerative options. Although minor disruptions still occurred within this system (e.g., with "visiting sheriffs" during holidays), this was minimal compared with the flux and inconsistency of District Court systems.

Involvement with Sheriff Courts (High Courts) may offer the most promising system for development of AEC services. The high level of consistency and reliability of these systems could offer rewarding environments for subsequent development of new initiatives.

Deferred Sentences and Probation Orders

Within the national pattern of AEC services, 25% of agencies provided courses via deferred sentencing, whereas 75% offered AECs as a condition of probation/probation order (Gamba et al., 1989). This may indicate a shift of emphasis toward more use of deferred sentencing since a previous survey (Baldwin & Heather, 1987) and less use of probation sentencing.

Possible advantages of conditions of attendance via probation may include increased attendance probabilities, increased credibility, more accountability by AEC staff, more clarity by clients about expectations, and viable numbers for AECs. Despite these claims, however, counterarguments for voluntarism within probation orders have been identified (McLoone et al., 1986). In particular: attendance at AECs can be achieved within existing probation orders; compulsory attendance AECs should not necessarily be viewed as an alternative to custody; course contents should be a greater incentive to attend than a threat of breach proceedings; and conditions of probation become superfluous when people decide they want to alter their behavior.

This is consistent with the belief that educational drinking interventions with offender/clients should be noncoercive and without the threat of compulsion (McGuire & Priestley, 1985). In effect, this decision to provide AEC interventions only for clients who wish to modify their drinking/offending behaviors may restrict availability to a small subpopulation of all offender/clients with drinking problems.

Thus, while AECs might be of potential benefit to many offender/clients, only some will opt for a course. This decision to accept an AEC option may occur at source (i.e., in the court) or during the MSI assessment; if "problem recognition" has not produced a decision to take action (Prochaska & Di Clemente, 1982) then the offender probably will reject the AEC option and continue with existing drinking/offending styles.

AECs based on a deferred sentence from the courts might be viewed as preferable to probation sentencing, as it is a less coercive sentencing option. Although this theme has been central to the debate about use of deferred sentencing or probation options, no empirical analysis of outcomes has been completed. The subjective opinions of offender/clients have included both views: some have expressed negative feelings about a sentence that is "hanging over them" and prefer to "get it over with"; others have reported preferences for deferred sentences rather than probation orders because they have "felt more in control" and felt more responsibility for their own behavior.

No single AEC option will meet the needs of all offender/clients. Rational decisions about choice of interventions can be made only from empirical analyses of client outcomes. Matching of AEC interventions to individual client needs remains a fruitful area for subsequent investigations.

Cost Effectiveness

Cost effectiveness considerations may include speed, scope, and durability of interventions as well as total costs of services to clients, families, and society. They may also include costs to therapists/counselors from education and training as well as availability and acceptability to clients (Parlott, 1986). Such calculations should include calculations of cost offset; this might include reduced uptake in other areas, such as social work services.

AECs may assist some offender/clients toward reform of drinking/offending behaviors. As a group-based intervention for young offenders, it may provide a cost effective intervention for a "special needs" population that frequently does not receive many resources/funding.

Summary

As an alternative to custodial sentencing, AECs may offer a cost effective option for a subpopulation of clients whose offending behaviors do not create high personal risk/danger to other persons; clients with rules/regulations and property offenses may be primary candidates for such interventions. In a criminal justice system that has been severely overloaded, and in the context of constraints on custodial options of unproven reform potential, provision of noninstitutional AECs may be a highly cost effective sentencing alternative.

11

Conclusions

Research Overview

Establishment and maintenance of AECs has been the subject of investment of much time, money, and staffing among fieldwork practitioners in the United Kingdom. This activity has been continued without any data on effectiveness to support such service provision. In particular, information-based AECs (modal type) have been provided in the knowledge that their effects on drug-taking behaviors are equivocal at best. Several factors may have contributed to this situation, including lack of funds for evaluation, deficits of skills among practitioners, and pressure to provide services rather than to evaluate them. Also, there has been a failure among funding agencies and researchers to make the alcohol/offending interface a priority for investment.

By definition, all AECs have focused on change of individual offender/clients to impact on subsequent drinking/offending problems. The focus of change has been explicitly directed at the individual offender/client rather than directed toward the environments that clients inhabit or toward society (that produces both clients and their environments). Thus, whereas some types of AEC may achieve modest positive improvements among some clients, most eligible clients are not referred for AECs; such courses may be completed by 5% to 10% of clients who could benefit from such an intervention.

This low overall success rate among the whole population of drunken offenders suggests that other interventions might be explored.

Other Courses

In addition to AEC provision, offender/clients may benefit from other short skills-based courses (e.g., Spence, 1979; Spence & Marzillier, 1981). Provision of problem-specific, client-specific interventions based on controlled evaluations may provide a useful focus for future research. Specificity of course contents to meet the particular needs of offenders has been recommended to improve "matching" and selectivity of interventions to clients (e.g., Blackburn, 1980). In addition, subsequent evaluations might focus on the "best available strategy" (O'Leary & Borkovec, 1978). Specifically, behavioral AECs might be compared with information-based AECs. Improved methodologies with more specific research questions would ask which intervention is best for each particular problem, client, and therapist (Beutler, 1979; Paul, 1976).

Court Interventions

Given the limitations for behavior change among individuals, however, and the dimensions of problems among the total population of offenders, AECs may have limited potency. As a method of social control, AECs help some individual offenders to reduce the intensity or frequency of their problem behaviors. Problems with referral rates in many courts, however, have blocked progress. In particular, despite some local exceptions (e.g., Menary, 1988), many courts have been slow to refer clients for such interventions.

Thus, whereas to date all AEC initiatives have been focused on the behavior of individual offender/clients, future services might consider the potential offered by interventions aimed at courts and court officials. The empirically derived observations from the present study support this shift of aims to a different level of intervention.

Specifically, future initiatives might be directed toward modification of individual court officials and their sentencing behavior toward offender/clients. Although such interventions may produce some ethical dilemmas (e.g., manipulation of social agencies and their staff), the payoffs for offender/client may justify such methods. Some recent initiatives have been quite promising (e.g., prior screening by court staff of offenders who have alcohol problems), although methodological barriers have not yet been resolved (e.g., Kilshaw, 1987).

Drinking/Offending Environments

Some AECs offer an intervention for offenders who have drinking problems but this idiographic approach does not meet the challenge to modify drinking/offending environments. The knowledge that personal characteristics account for only between 30% and 50% of the total variance of the person/environment interface raises the question of modification of situational influences on drinking and offending behaviors.

In particular, attempts have been made to "design out crime" from specific environments via a range of physical modifications (Clarke, 1983). These have included surveillance studies (Kelling & Pate, 1981; Larson, 1975), "target hardening" (Heller, Sterzel, Gill, Kilde, & Schimerman, 1975); and environmental management (Mayhew, Clarke, Sturman, & Hough, 1976). Some initiatives have been directed specifically to modify the alcohol/offending interface (e.g., provision of plastic containers in pubs where fights occur; Scottish Council on Crime, 1975). Detailed behavioral analyses of environmental settings (Stumphauzer, Veloz, &

Aiken, 1981) may assist with the identification of neighborhoods that increase probabilities of offending behavior.

Implementation problems, however, and secondary consequences of environmental manipulations (e.g., crime displacement), have retarded establishment and subsequent evaluation of these initiatives (e.g., Clarke, 1983). Moreover, specific contingencies operate as powerful variables to reduce opportunities for environmental manipulations. For example, although reductions in total number of retail outlets or in licensing hours might reduce opportunities for public drunkenness offending behavior, such reductions are unlikely because of extraneous variables that exert opposite effects (i.e., to increase licensing hours and retail outlets) (Cuthbert, 1988).

In addition, more overt manipulations of environments may produce shifts in the incidence of problem behaviors such as drinking and offending. Preliminary work completed with behavioral analysis of individual neighborhoods has produced a method for data collection based on systematic attention to motivational analysis, developmental analysis, self-control, relationships, and physical environments (Stumphauzer, 1981).

Social/Cultural Variables

Despite the impact of some AECs on the drinking/offending behavior of some individuals, most offender/clients in the United Kingdom do not have access to such interventions. In addition, the overall effects of AECs on offender/clients may be restricted as a "secondary prevention" method, when compared to what might be achieved via broad changes in social policy or legislation (Bunton, 1988). Moreover, incidence of alcohol/offending problems among teenagers and young adults may be affected directly by variables such as: (a) pricing, (b) outlets, (c) advertising campaigns, (d) penal codes (e.g., penalties/sanctions), or (e) policing. Some successes have been achieved from specific local schemes (e.g., more effective policing of alcohol policy; Jeffs & Saunders, 1983). In practice, however, it is extremely difficult to obtain access and control of such variables. Thus, the popularity of AECs may be explained by a partial failure to gain control of these other social policy/legislation variables.

Funding for Evaluations

In surveys, many AEC fieldworkers who did not evaluate their services cited funding problems as the major single reason that their service remained unevaluated. Most AEC fieldworkers also believed that extra staffing was required to initiate evaluations of their services.

Although extra financing and staffing can be helpful in establishing evaluation procedures, however, these are not prerequisite additions. Service-based evaluations can be started by fieldworkers, with no additional resource provision. This does require practitioners, however, to redefine their professional roles and responsibilities.

Since 1981, AEC services have flourished in the United Kingdom, despite absence of data on effectiveness. While actual costings for these services are unknown, these have been estimated at not less than £15 million (Greer, Baldwin, Lawson, & Cochrane, 1990). The total budget for AEC evaluations since 1981 has been less than £100,000 (less than 1% of revenue costs). Although this discrepancy between research and practice is not unusual, it has highlighted the "blind faith" adherence to the prevailing ideology in social work/probation services that alcohol education is a "good thing." This belief in the zeitgeist may have obscured the exploration and evaluation of other noncustodial sentencing options. Despite some innovative alternative training programs, most services have been developed according to a traditional format.

Other Funding Sources

Whereas many social work/probation agencies have supported AEC service provision via staffing or equipment, a similar commitment to evaluation has not occurred, despite the effort of local initiatives (e.g., Stevens, 1986). Given the pervasiveness of unevaluated services in this field (Gamba et al., 1989), a shift toward effectiveness studies will be difficult to achieve.

At national level, funding from research councils in the field have been targeted on three individual projects rather than distributed equally between many projects. This pattern has been most helpful in assisting several specific projects to move toward evaluation of local services. Nonetheless, at least two undesirable outcomes of this funding pattern have occurred: (a) a pervasive passivity among practitioners who wish to be informed by an "expert researcher" and (b) development of services that are only committed to provision and not to an examination of effectiveness. One possible outcome of such service delivery systems is that original goals (e.g., "rehabilitation") can be submerged underneath a new agenda (Praill & Baldwin, 1988).

Funds from national research councils for effectiveness evaluations of AECs are unlikely to be made available without considerable investments of time and resources; even these efforts will be limited by the perceived low status of research with offenders who have drinking problems. In addition, alcohol education campaigns that are effective in reducing alcohol consumption are unlikely to be funded anyway (Smith, 1982).

Although fieldwork research with drinking offenders may be of value to the client group, it is not viewed as an area for priority funding within the research environment. Such applied research generally will achieve only low status because of its focus on nonscientific consumers (Rieken & Boruch, 1974). Research with drinking offenders may suffer from additional negative imagery. A shift from this position would require a fundamental reappraisal of societal values, and convincing demonstrations of possible benefits from interventions with offenders who have drinking problems.

Evaluation Methodology

The utility of much previous research in the alcohol/offending field has been limited by fundamental design flaws such as inadequate controls for experimental groups (Blackburn, 1980; Greenberg, 1982). Even some of the more robust studies have been restricted by problems of generalizability because of small sample size (e.g., Spence, 1979; Spence & Marzillier, 1981). In summary, much research at the alcohol/offending interface has been characterized by insufficient attention to experimental design, maintenance, generalizability, and durability. Moreover, many previous studies have lacked sufficient attention to specific client characteristics such as sex, SES, education, employment status, race, interview location, interview method, and interview characteristics. In addition, the unknown reliability of self-report measures increases the need to introduce more robust measures of alcohol consumption in field settings. In particular, alcohol consumption sampled at random from the natural environment would provide more direct measures of specific behavior (Kazdin, 1978).

In particular, such summative evaluations have required demonstrations of causal inference based on a cause-effect relationship; that variations in "causes" precede variations in "effects," and that no alternative explanations are possible. The achievement of statistical conclusion validity will require demonstration of validity of the conclusions about statistical associations between presumed "causes" and "effects." Previous research often has failed to account for the influence of type I and type II errors, based on "false positives" and "false negatives" (Cook, et al., 1977). In addition, accounts of fieldwork interventions have neglected to discuss external validity (generalizability to new persons, times, and settings) or internal validity (determination of causal relationships).

Specific design features have been identified to increase statistical conclusion validity, including (a) large sample sizes, (b) decreased extraneous sources of error (standard measurements, homogeneous populations, (c) accounting for extraneous sources of variance in statistical analyses, (d) increasing reliability of outcome measures, and (e) standardizing intervention implementation (Cook et al., 1977).

Current Research

The present evaluation research was designed to address these topics. All studies were designed to meet minimum criteria for evaluation research in crime and delinquency: (a) adequate definition of behavioral program, (b) routinization of techniques (e.g., via manualization), (c) random division into intervention and control groups, (d) evidence that intervention group had received the defined intervention, (e) "before and after" measures, (f) definition of "success" and "failure" of program, and (g) follow-up for control and intervention groups (Logan, 1972). True control groups were used when possible, with attention to random allocation and use of a single-blind design. Limitations of field settings, however, exerted major restrictions on ideal designs because of difficulties in manipulation of variables in forensic settings. A quasi-experimental design also was used, and this reduced the potency of some research findings and exerted limits on representativeness.

Problems of small sample sizes occurred in all experimental studies; while recruitment and follow-up difficulties were minimized in a secure custodial environment, evaluation research in this setting raised several ethical questions. Intractable problems of recruitment and follow-up may be a joint function of general difficulties of "positive valuation" of controlled drinking programs and perception of "appropriateness" of interventions with offenders. Recruitment of large numbers of clients into AEC evaluation research programs may require overt manipulation of several contingencies in court settings to overcome system resistance to such evaluation attempts.

Some client characteristics did not apply in the present research (e.g., race; all clients were white males) although such an unrepresentative cohort indicates the use of exclusion/discrimination criteria by forensic systems. Some variables that might be expected to influence outcome did not exert such effects (e.g., SES, educational level, employment status). There was, however, some evidence that some clients who had completed behavioral AECs had made changes in other areas of their life (e.g., housing, relationships, employment). This may suggest some generalization of skills into other settings, although this evidence has remained anecdotal.

MSI interviews were completed in local Council on Alcohol premises or at social work departments. Follow-up interviews were completed in a range of locations, including clients' residences and local cafes as well as the above settings. Interview location did not affect outcome or quality of data; location choices were based on client preferences. The only interview method used was the MSI; although validity and reliability measures were not completed, it was based on a previously published instrument (Marlatt & Miller, 1984).

The MSI provided a highly structured interview schedule to obtain information about drinking and offending behaviors. It required research interviewers to adopt a standard approach with clients and discouraged interviewers from working with clients' problems.

Thus, while the MSI provided much structure and a standard format for presentation, it did not include open-ended questions that allowed clients to discuss their problems. The MSI was designed to obtain information rather than to provide a diagnostic instrument. As a reliable method of making assessments about appropriate referrals for AECs, however, the MSI was effective; it seemed helpful in enabling "contemplative clients" to move into an action stage. It seemed less effective at moving clients from "precontemplation" to "contemplation"; clients who did not believe or recognize that their drinking was a problem required a more powerful intervention to produce this shift.

Many clients, for example, stated they would need to be drinking *every day* before their drinking was "a problem." This cultural stereotype was powerful and pervasive. Other studies have reported similar findings of this belief system among young delinquents, which reflects powerful distortions (e.g., "only older people can be problem drinkers") (Stumphauzer, 1980).

Future Research

The major single challenge for future research is to implement controlled evaluations in existing field settings. While the establishment of new AEC services could offer opportunities to develop more "ideal" service systems, excessive time is required for such an enterprize; the benefits of establishment of new services are outweighed by the disadvantages incurred from time delays. Instead, future research initiatives should be directed at controlled evaluations of existing AECs, either in partnership with practitioners, or agreed via a consultancy role. While new research projects would have a higher probability of obtaining funds, the priority should be to build research initiatives into existing AEC services.

AECs may impact on some offender/client populations to reduce drinking/offending behaviors but some data have indicated the potency of a "minimal intervention based on interview-only" techniques. The potent role of such techniques has been demonstrated repeatedly with other drinking populations (Babor, Ritson, & Hodgson, 1986; Miller, 1985; Miller & Hester, 1986; Miller et al., 1988; Ritson, 1986). Similarly some positive changes on drinking behavior have been reported at 3-month follow-up from similar "minimal intervention" techniques based on provision of self-help manuals (McMurran & Boyle, 1989). Such interventions, based on a distillation of larger components, may be promising research areas for the future.

In addition, design problems require resolution; even single-site, single intervention experiments designed to achieve a single objective produce major challenges when applied to populations of young drinking offenders. The implementation of multisite, alternative version interventions that depend on practitioner skills (Rieken & Boruch, 1974) may be inappropriate to the design problem.

Other than funding, the main barrier to implementation of AEC services will be the difficulty of manipulation of court officials to cooperate with a research protocol. In particular, major obstacles would be likely from establishment of: (a) no-intervention control groups, (b) randomized allocation to interventions, and (c) large numbers of referrals of offender/clients.

Such objections have been common in the domain of policy evaluation. Three barriers have recurred in applied settings: (a) impracticality of introduction of experimental procedures in applied action research setting, (b) inability of experimental design procedures to evaluate total policy, and (c) limited generalizability of results (Scioli & Cook, 1975).

Surmounting barriers to implementation of controlled evaluation designs in AEC services will require strategic solutions. Specifically, ethical objections to no-intervention control groups should be acknowledged; equally, however, the continued provision of unevaluated services also should be viewed as morally questionable (West, 1980). On balance, it may be less objectionable to include no-intervention control groups as part of a scientific evaluation than to commit the service to nonevaluation.

Future nomothetic research based on cumulative evaluations should attend to more rigorous design methodologies to increase validity (Cook et al., 1977).

Specifically, evaluators should attend to (a) increased external validity (random selection, heterogeneous groups, generalization), (b) increased construct validity (demonstration that the intervention varied only what it was supposed to vary), and (c) increased internal validity (exclusion of history, maturation, statistical regression, selection, interactions).

Future initiatives also should question the continued commitment to an idiographic research perspective. The underlying hypothesis about the "model of change" based on the reform of individual offenders has been challenged (Prins, 1980). In particular, radical criminologists have maintained that problems exist in society and not in individual offenders, and that attempts by clinicians to reform such clients will be wasteful. Moreover, such attempts could be harmful because of diverted attention from social system defects (West, 1980). In addition, evaluators should reconcile such attempts with outcome research studies that find little or no difference in effectiveness between psychotherapies. Future research might examine (a) equivalence of outcome, (b) equivalence of content, and (c) equivalence of mechanism (Stiles, et al., 1986). Also, subsequent reports of outcome research in the field should present data in sufficient detail to allow incorporation into meta-analysis research.

Other observers have criticized the underlying model and methodology of such evaluations (Hudson, 1977). The assumption of a simple linear relationship between program, process, and outcomes may be invalid in this context. Other models may better explain the phenomenon, including curvilinear relationships or nonlinear step functions, which show no effects until a particular value has been reached. Thus, research studies may show no significant relationship between interventions and outcomes despite a large potential effect. This has produced a focus on the matching of particular types of clients to particular interventions. Improved measurement techniques are required to avoid the potential masking of differential program effects on clients.

Specifically, the proposition of problem resolution via acquisition of new knowledge or skills has been viewed as naive (Grant, 1982), inappropriate (Cuthbert, 1988), or of limited potency. A more sophisticated understanding of teenage and adult drinking behavior will require a focus on how this population "learns not to drink" (e.g., Stumphauzer, 1980, 1982, 1983, 1986).

Therefore, as a parallel development to the increased evaluation of existing AECs, other research initiatives might be directed at empirical investigations of court-based interventions (e.g., manipulation of court officials) or intervention with social policy/procedures (e.g., field experiments following legislation changes). Similarly, other points of entry should be considered for modification attempts, including law enforcement systems and neighborhoods (Davidson & Seidman, 1974). Although these developments also provide major barriers to implementation, they merit the focus of research enquiry.

AEC interventions in penal institutions have provided a special challenge for alcohol educators and researchers. With some evidence to support the effectiveness of an AEC for prerelease young offenders in a penal institution, the evaluation of similar initiatives should remain a high priority for agency staff (McMurran &

Baldwin, 1989). While penal settings produce many barriers to in vivo modification of drinking/offending behaviors, some recent developments have yielded some promising local initiatives (e.g., establishment of a bar serving non alcohol drinks in a YOI setting) (McMurran, 1988). Such modifications of problem drinking behaviors via "cue exposure" has an established pedigree in the field (Hodgson & Rankin, 1976, 1982; Hodgson et al., 1978; Hodgson, Stockwell, & Rankin, 1979), and have been applied in other institutional settings (Rankin, Hodgson, & Stockwell, 1983).

Such research, although difficult, represents a major challenge for the future. This exploration of nomothetic variables would complement the present idiographic focus on individuals. In particular, an examination of political initiatives is overdue. These include regular increase on alcohol tax to maintain real price, bans on alcohol advertizing, reduction in numbers of alcohol outlets, tighter laws on drunken driving (e.g., random breath testing), and a ban on further loosening of licensing laws (Smith, 1982).

Alcohol Education

Within the wider context of drug education, alcohol education (as a "secondary prevention" strategy for young offenders with drinking problems) has been a predominant alternative to custodial sentencing. It has been developed within the United Kingdom as a main component of service delivery in social work and probation, despite the absence of a "design template." Despite major limitations of design, implementation, and evaluation, AECs have flourished and have become "institutionalized" into many forensic services. At least, AECs have increased the probability of noncustodial sentencing of several thousand offenders.

Future Status

Empirical evidence about alcohol (or other drug) education has been equivocal at best (Kim, Hoffman, & Pike, 1984; Moore & Weiss, 1985). With some licit and illicit substances, "education" (i.e., information) may precipitate subsequent drug usage. In addition, alcohol and drug education fields have been operating for too long without use of mainstream knowledge from health education (Winick, 1980, 1985). The status of "alcohol education courses" within this context requires a careful consideration. In particular, it may set the conditions for other controlled evaluations of interventions that consider multiple substance abuse among offender/clients (Miller & Welte, 1987).

In particular, the continued provision of unevaluated information-based AECs could be counterproductive in a climate where offender/clients become sensitized to education attempts (Bagnall & Plant, 1987). Lack of attention to adequate follow-up of drinking/offending behaviors after AEC completion may mask negative outcomes. Furthermore, continued provision of information-based AECs is not supported by present research findings. Adaptive behavioral changes in drinking/offending behaviors occurred following completion of behavioral AECs by some clients: institutionalized offenders, in particular, had gained from AEC completion at follow-up.

Possible implications for other aspects of drug education suggests that "information provision" alone will be insufficient to produce desired behavior changes. Although not a novel finding, this suggests that programs aimed at other client groups within the field of addictions (e.g., intravenous drug injectors) require more than information provision in posters and leaflets. Specifically, such client groups may require specific skills acquisition to reduce or eliminate high-risk behaviors (e.g., needle sharing). Whereas information provision may be the first step of an "education" campaign, it may be wholly inadequate to achieve reform of high-risk behaviors. This possibility has major implications for public education initiatives (e.g., AIDS campaign) aimed at behavior change among at-risk individuals.

Measures of Change

Most AEC fieldworkers who collect follow-up data report measures based on behavioral observations, either drinking or offending. Reliance on "reoffending" measures such as reconviction data has been criticized as vague and ambiguous as an indication of "recidivism" (Hudson, 1977). The imprecision of outcomes and the indirect measures may restrict the utility of this approach in forensic settings.

In addition, most research interventions with offender/clients have relied on indirect methods of recording not based on direct observation of discrete behaviors. Similarly, while there have been some local exceptions (e.g., Menary, 1986), most agents have not used applied interventions in natural settings. Ethical barriers have prevented interventions that include modification of actual drinking behavior using alcohol (i.e., cue exposure) (Hodgson & Rankin, 1976; Rankin et al., 1983).

Some AEC fieldworkers also have used "cognitive" measures such as "attitudes to alcohol," although these observations are less common (Baldwin & Heather, 1987; Gamba et al., 1989). To date, fieldworkers have not used physiological measures as part of a battery assessment of change. Although there have been some reports of "alcometers" on AECs (e.g., Harding, 1986), these have provided only limited information about BALs/BACs.

The lack of physiological measures in AECs has been a major limitation in the field. Specifically, an over-reliance on behavioral and cognitive variables has produced a bias against investigation of physiological/biochemical concomitants of change. In practice, this has slanted research enquiry away from "hard data" investigations in favor of measures based on less invasive techniques (Pallone, 1988). With the exception of collateral data and corroborative data from forensic sources, most AEC fieldwork has been based on completion of self-report materials (e.g., drink diaries). Such single-source material may have major limitations on reliability and validity (Midanik, 1982). One challenge for AEC fieldwork and research will be to incorporate physiological measures into future projects to complete the spectrum of multimodal personal assessment.

The achievement of research data that are reliable, durable, and replicable will require incorporation of multisource reporting techniques, corroborative data, and resolution of self-report reliability problems. While technological methods may be limited by cost implications, remote sensing techniques may provide one alternative.

Alcohol Education Courses and Sentencing Policy

Despite the national expansion of AECs in the United Kingdom since 1981, no data on effectiveness have been produced. Rapid developments of AEC services in local settings have not been matched by a commitment to evaluation. Moreover, many Magistrates Courts in England and Wales have been persuaded to refer clients to AECs; only before-after data, however, have been collected in support of such schemes.

National surveys of offender/clients referred to AECs have provided evidence of substantial support in some courts for such noncustodial alternatives for drunkenness offending (Gamba et al., 1989). While some AECs may not reduce drinking/offending behaviors (and may in fact potentiate some similar behaviors), these services have continued to expand. One explanation for such expansion (in the absence of supportive data) is that human services planning and development are not based on empirical study (Praill & Baldwin, 1988). Another explanation may be that court officials have been forced to consider noncustodial sentencing alternatives as a response to overcrowded prisons and ineffective fining practices. Use of AECs as a noncustodial alternative may not reflect a positive decision about this option as much as a negative decision about existing options.

The Paradigm Shift

Increased use of controlled evaluations will increase the probability of provision of data on "information-based" AECs. Such data may not support claims for effectiveness in modifying drinking/offending behaviors. This outcome eventually may reduce the usage of AECs as a noncustodial option. Alternatively, it may increase the probability that AEC contents become more behavioral and less based on information provision.

One possible delay in this paradigm shift (Kuhn, 1962) to a new conceptual model may be the confusion that surrounds the terminology of AECs. Such alcohol education initiatives have been known locally as alcohol education courses (Robertson & Heather, 1982), alcohol education programs (Stevens, 1986), alcohol study groups (Singer, 1983), alcohol edcuation group (AIC, 1982), and alcohol education project (Home Office, 1982).

Resolution of this confusion may be enhanced by the recognition that effective courses are based on *skills acquisition:* Alcohol/Offending Skills Group (AOSG) may better define the nature, content, and function of future initiatives for offender/clients who have drinking problems. The empirical question would then be to determine whether formal recognition of the true nature of such groups would impact on the referral behavior of court officials. Future research might test the hypothesis that explicit provision of skills-based courses to modify drinking and offending behaviors might decrease the probability of referral by court officials. Specifically, probability of referral may be inversely related to potency of intervention.

Bibliography

Abelson, H. I. Fishburne, P. M. & Cisin, I. (1977). *National survey on drug abuse* (Vol. 1) Main Findings Response Analysis. Princeton, New Jersey.

Addeo, E. G. & Addeo, J. R. (1975). *Why our children drink.* Prentice Hall. Englewood Cliffs, New Jersey.

Ahlstrom, S. (1985). Study of alcohol related problems in young people. Paper for W.H.O. European Regional Office, Stockholm.

AIC (1982). Coventry Alcohol Education Group. Alcoholism Information Centre, Coventry.

Akers, R. L. & Krohn, M. D. Lanza-Kaduce, L. Rodosevich, M. (1979). Social learning and deviant behavior: A specific test of general therapy. *American Sociological Review, 44,* 635/655.

Babor, T. F. Ritson, E. B. & Hodgson, R. J. (1986). Alcohol related problems in the primary health care setting: A review of early intervention strategies. *British Journal of Addiction, 81,* 23/46.

Bagnall, G. & Plant, M. (1987). Adolescent drinking. *British Journal of Addiction, 82,* 829/830.

Bailey, H. & Purser, R. (1982). Coventry Alcohol Education Group. West Midlands Probation Service, Coventry.

Bailey, M. B. S. & Tennant, O. (1967). Normal drinking by persons reporting previous problem drinking. *Quarterly Journal of Studies on Alcohol, 28,* 305/315.

Bailey, W. C. (1966). Correctional outcome: An evaluation of 100 reports. *The Journal of Criminal Law, Criminology and Police Science, 57,* (2), 153/160.

Baldwin, S. Braggins, F. Heather, N. Lawson, A. Masters, G. Mooney, J. & Robertson, I. (1991). Comparison of behavioural and talk-based alcohol education courses. (Manuscript submitted for publication).

Baldwin, S. Gamba, S. Heather, N. Lawson, A. & Robertson, I. (1991). Comparison of alcohol education course effectiveness in urban and rural settings. (Manuscript submitted for publication).

Baldwin, S. Cuthbert, J. Greer, C. McCluskey, S. & Lawson, A. (1991). Effectiveness of an alcohol education course for young offenders in urban courts. (Manuscript submitted for publication).

Baldwin, S. Ford, I. & Heather, N. (1987). Drink and crime. *Community Care,* April 2. 12/13.

Baldwin, S. Ford, I. Heather, N. & Braggins, F. (1987). Drink and crime II. *Community Care.* April 9. 22/23.

Baldwin, S. Greer, C. & Gamba, S. (1991). Therapeutic outcomes for individuals court-ordered for interventions. (Manuscript submitted for publication).

Baldwin, S. Greer, C. Heather, N. Robb, E. Robertson, I. Ward, M. & Williams, A. (1991). Effectiveness of pre-release alcohol education courses for young offenders in a penal institution. (Manuscript submitted for publication).

Baldwin, S. & Heather, N. (1987). Alcohol education courses and offenders: Survey of 20 U.K. agencies. *Alcohol and Alcoholism. 22,* (11), 79/82.

Baldwin, S. Lawson, A. & Mooney, J. (1991). Alcohol education course for offenders: Five year follow-up. (Manuscript submitted for publication).

Baldwin, S. & Thomson, D. (1991). A court-based intervention to regulate referrals for alternative sentencing schemes. (Manuscript submitted for publication).

Baldwin, S. Wilson, M. Lancaster, A. & Allsop, D. (1988). Ending Offending: An alcohol training resource pack for people working with young offenders. Glasgow. Scottish Council on Alcohol.

Baldwin, S. Wilson, M. Lancaster, A. Allsop McGowan, T. D. McMurran, M. & Hodge, J. (1989). Ending Offending 2: Alcohol education course for young offenders in secure settings. Glasgow. Scottish Council on Alcohol.

Balfour-Sclare, A. (1985). Treatment of alcoholism in Scotland. *International Journal of Offender Therapy and Comparative Criminology, 17.* 153/165.

Basham, R. B. (1986). Scientific and practical advantages of comparative design in psychotherapy outcome research. *Journal of Consulting and Clinical Psychology,* 54, (1), 88/94.

Bender, M. (1976). *Community Psychology.* London. Methuen.

Berk, R. A. & Brewer, M. (1977). Feet of clay in hobnail boots: An assessment of statistical inference in applied research. Unpublished manuscript.

Bernstein, D. A. (1973). Behavioural fear assessment: Anxiety or artifact? In H. Adams & I.P. Unikel (Eds.), *Issues and trends in behavior therapy.* Springfield, Illinois. C. C. Thomas.

Beutler, L. E. (1979). Toward specific psychological therapies for specific conditions. *Journal of Consulting and Clinical Psychology, 47,* 882/897.

Biddle, B. J. Bank, B. J. & Martin, M. M. (1980). Social determinants of adolescent drinking: What they think, what they do, and what I think they do. *Journal of Studies on Alcohol,* 14, (3), 213/241.

Blackburn, R. (1980). Still not working? A look at recent outcomes in offender rehabilitation. Paper presented at Scottish branch of the British Psychological Society Conference on "Deviance." University of Stirling.

Blackburn, R. (1985). Cognitive-behavioural approaches to understanding and treating aggression and violence. University of Leicester. Unpublished manuscript.

Blane, T. S. (1976). Education and Prevention of Alcoholism. In B. Kismi & H. Begleiter (Eds.), *The biology of alcoholism—social aspects of alcoholism.* (Vol. 4). New York. Plenum Press.

Blomqvist, J. & Holmberg, R. (1988). Appropriate treatment for each client. A research project aimed at an analysis of the grounds for treatment selection and at developing and evaluating a model for matching clients with treatment. Paper presented at 35th International Congress on Alcoholism and Drug Dependence, Oslo.

Brody, S. R. (1976). The effectiveness of sentencing—A review of the literature. Home Office Research Study, No. 35. London. HMSO.

Brunswick, A. F. (1979). Black youth and drug use behavior. In G. Beschner & A. Friedman (Eds.), *Youth, drug abuse: Problems, issues and treatment.* Lexington, Massachusetts. Lexington Books.

Bruun, K. (1966). The polar bear approach to alcoholism. Proceedings of 12th International Institute on the Prevention and Treatment of Alcoholism, Prague.

Bruun, K. Edwards, G. Lunio, M. Makela, K. Pan, K. Popham, R.E. Room, R. Schmidt, W. Skog, O. Sulkenen, P. & Osterberg, E. (1975). Alcohol control policies in the public health perspective. Finnish Foundation for Alcohol Studies, 25, Finland.

Bunton, R. (1988). Prevention as social control: Some issues in the public health perspective. Paper presented at New Directions in the Study of Alcohol Group Annual Conference, University of Cambridge.

Cahalan, E. & Room, R. (1974). Problem drinking among American men, *Monograph 7*. New Brunswick, New Jersey: Rutgers Centenary Alcohol Studies.

Camberwell Council on Alcoholism (1968). New Society, 295, 756.

Cameron, D. & Spence, M.T. (1976). Lessons from an outpatient controlled drinking group. *Journal of Alcoholism, II*, 44/45.

Campbell, D. T. & Stanley, J. C. (1963). *Experimental and quasi-experimental designs for research.* Chicago. Rand McNally.

Celanto, D. S. & McQueen, D. V. (1978) Comparison of alcoholism prevalence rates obtained by survey and indirect estimators. *Journal of Studies on Alcohol, 39*, 420/434.

Chafetz, M. E. (1971). In alcohol and health. Special Report to the US Congress. DHEW Publication No. (HSM) 72/9099.

Clarke, R. V. (1983). Situational crime prevention: Its theoretical basis and practical scope. In M. Tonry, & N. Morris, (Eds.), *Crime and Justice: An annual review of research.* (Vol. 4). Chicago. University of Chicago Press.

Clayton, R. R. & Ross, H. L. (1977). Shacking up: Cohabitation in the 1970s. *Journal of Marriage and Families, 39*, 273/283.

Cohen, J. (1962). The statistical power of abnormal-social psychological research. *Journal of Abnormal and Social Psychology, 65*, (3), 145/153.

Collins, J. J. (1982). *Drinking and crime.* New York. Guilford Press.

Collins, S. A. & Tate, D. H. (1988). Alcohol-related offenders and a voluntary organisation in a Scottish community. *The Howard Journal of Criminal Justice, 27*, (1), 44/57.

Cook, T. D. & Campbell, T. D. (1976). The design and conduct of quasi-experiments and true experiments in field settings. In M. Dunnet (Ed.), *Handbook of industrial and organisational psychology.* Chicago. Rand McNally.

Cook, T. D. & Campbell, D. T. (1979). *Quasi-experimentation: Design and analysis issues for field settings.* Chicago. Rand McNally.

Cook, T. D, Cook, F. L. & Mark, M. M. (1977). Random and quasi-experimental designs in evaluation research: An introduction. In L. Rutman (Ed.), *Evaluation research methods: A basic guide.* Beverley Hills. Sage.

Cook, T. Morgan, H. G. & Pollak, B. (1968). *British Medical Journal, 1*, 240.

Crawshaw, A. (1990). Personal communication.

Cuthbert, J. (1988). Personal communication.

Davidson, W. S. & Robinson, M. J. (1975). Community psychology and behavior modification: A community-based program for the prevention of delinquency. *Journal of Corrective Psychiatry and Behavior Therapy, 21*, 1/12.

Davidson, W. S. & Seidman, E. (1974). Studies of behavior modification and juvenile delinquency: A review, methodological critique, and social perspective. *Psychological Bulletin, 81*, (12), 998/1011.

Davies, D. L. (1962). Normal drinking in recovered alcohol addicts. *Quarterly Journal of the Studies on Alcohol, 23*, 94/104.

Dight, S. E. (1976). Scottish drinking habits. London. HMSO

Driver, R. J. (1969). The United States Supreme Court and the chronic drunkenness offender. *Quarterly Journal of Studies on Alcohol, 30*, 165/172.

Duncan, C. P. O'Brien, R. B. Murray, D. C. Davis, L. & Gilliard, A. R. (1957). Some information about a test of psychological misconceptions. *Journal of General Psychology, 56,* 257/260.

Dunkin, W. S. (1981). Policies in the United States. In B. D. Hore & M. A. Plant, (Eds.), *Alcohol problems in employment.* London. Croom Helm.

Duryea, E. J. (1983). Utilizing tenets of innoculation theory to develop and evaluate a preventative alcohol education intervention. *Journal of School Health, 53,* (4), 250/256.

Education Commission of the USA (1978) Task force on responsible decisions about alcohol: A technical document. Denver, Colorado.

Edwards, G. (1970). Place of treatment professions in society's response to chemical abuse. *British Medical Journal, ii,* 195/199.

Edwards, G. Grattoni, F. Hensman, C. & Peto, J. (1976). Drinking problems in prison populations. In G. Edwards et al. (Eds.), *Alcohol dependence and smoking behavior.* New York. Saxon House/Lexington Books.

Engs, R. C. (1982) Let's look before we leap: The cognitive and behavioral evaluation of a university alcohol education programme. *Journal of Alcohol and Drug Education, 22,* (2), 39/48.

Erikson, P. G. (1984). Diversion—A panacea for delinquency: Lessons from the Scottish experience. *Youth and Society, 16,* (1), 29/45.

Evans, C. M. (1980). Alcohol, violence and aggression. *British Journal of Alcohol and Alcoholism, 15,* 104.

Feldman, M. P. (1976). *Criminal behaviour,* London. Wiley.

Flay, B. R. & Sobell, J. L. (1983). Role of mass media in preventing adolescent substance abuse. *Research Monographs Series, 47,* 5-35 NIDA.

Fodor, I. E. (1972). The use of behavior-modification techniques with female delinquents. *Child Welfare, 51,* (2), February, 93/101.

Foucault, M. (1979). *Discipline and punishment. The birth of the prison.* Harmondsworth. Penguin.

Freeman, H. E. & Scott, J. F. (1966). A critical review of alcohol education for adolescents. *Community Mental Health Journal, 2,* 222/230.

Gamba, S. Baldwin, S. Greer, C. & McCluskey, S. (1989). Alcohol education courses and offenders: An update on UK services. *Alcohol and Alcoholism, 24,* (5), 473/478.

Gath, D. Hensman, C. Hawker, A. Kelly, M. & Edwards, G. (1968). The drunk in court: Survey of drunkenness offenders from two London courts. *British Medical Journal, 4,* 808/811.

Gayford, J. J. (1978). Wife battering: A preliminary survey of 100 cases. *British Medical Journal, 1,* 194/197.

Georgiades, N. J. & Phillimore, L. (1975). The myth of the hero-innovator. In C. C. Kiernan & F. P. Woodford (Eds.), *Behaviour modification with the severely retarded.* London. Associated Scientific Publishers.

Gibbons, T. & Silberman, M. (1970). Alcoholism amongst prisoners. *Psychological Medicine, 1,* 73/78.

Gillies, H. (1965). Murder in the west of Scotland. *British Journal of Psychiatry, 3,* 1087/1094.

Glaser, F. B. (1980). Anybody got a match? Treatment research and the matching hypothesis. In G. Edwards & M. Grant (Eds.), Alcoholism treatment in transition. London. Croom Helm.

Glaser, F. B. & Skinner, H. A. (1981). Matching in the real world: A practical approach. In E. Gottheil, A. T. McLellan, & K.A. Dury (Eds.), *Matching patient needs and treatment methods in alcoholism and drug abuse.* Springfield, Illinois. C. C. Thomas.

Godfrey, R. & Leahy, N. (1986) Education with the Probation Service. *Alcohol Concern, March, 2* (8), 17-19.

Gold, M. (1969) *Delinquent behavior in an American city.* Belmont, California. Brookes/Cole Publishing.

Gold, M. & Williams, J. R. (1969). National Study of the Aftermath of Apprehension. *Juvenile Delinquency Prospectus, December, 3,* (1), 3/12.

Goldberg, D. (1983). Mental illness in the community. London. Routledge.

Golbeth, G. (1975). An appraisal of drug education programs. In R. Gibbins, Y. Israel, H. Kalant, R. Popham, W. Schmidt & R. Smart (Eds.), *Research advances in alcohol and drug problems,* (Vol. 2). New York. John Wiley & Sons.

Goodman, P. & Scott, J. (1982). Trouble through drink: A probation response to drink-related offenders. *Probation Journal, 29,* 129/132.

Goodstadt, M. S. (1976). Drug education—Where do we go from here? In R. E. Ostman (Ed.), *Communication research and drug education.* Beverly Hills, California. Sage.

Goodstadt, M. S. (1978). Alcohol and drug education: Models and outcomes. *Health Education Monographs, Fall,* 263/279.

Grant, M. (1982). Alcohol education: Does it really affect drinking problems? *Journal of the Royal Society of Health, 102,* (5), 201/204.

Greenberg, S. W. (1982). Alcohol and Crime: A methodological critique of the literature. In J. J. Collins, (Ed.), *Drinking and crime.* New York. Guilford Press.

Greer, C. Baldwin, S. Lawson, A. & Gamba, S. (1990). Alcohol education courses and offenders: A policy review. (Manuscript submitted for publication).

Haberman, P. W. & Schienberg, J. (1969). Public attitudes towards alcoholism as an illness. *American Journal of Public Health, 59,* 1209/1216.

Hamilton, J. R. (1976). Helping the drunken offender. *Health and Social Services Journal, August 28,* 1550/1552.

Hamilton, J. R. Griffith, A. Ritson, E. B. & Aitken, R. C. B. (1977). The chief scientist reports...A detoxification unit for habitual drunken offenders. *Health and Social Services Journal, April 1,* 146/154.

Hanks, S. E. & Rosenbaum, C. D. (1977). Battered women: A study of women who live with violent alcohol-abusing men. *American Journal of Orthopsychiatry, 47,* 291/306.

Harding, J. (1986). Personal communication.

Harre, R. & Secord, P. F. (1972). *The explanation of social behaviour.* Oxford. Blackwell.

Hathaway, S. R. (1948). Some considerations relative to non-directive counselling as therapy. *Journal of Clinical Psychology, 4,* 226/231.

Hawker, A. & Stevenson, G. (1984). Young people, drink and the law: A descriptive study covering two London Magistrates' Courts. *Alcohol and Alcoholism, 19,* (1), 51/61.

Hawkins, R. O. (1982). Adolescent alcohol abuse: A review. *Developmental and Behavioral Paediatrics, 3,* (2), 83/87.

Heather, N. (1976). *Radical perspectives in psychology.* London. Methuen.

Heather, N. (1981). Relationships between delinquency and drunkenness among Scottish young offenders. *British Journal on Alcohol and Alcoholism, 16,* (2), 50/61.

Heather, N. (1982). Alcohol dependence and problem drinking in Scottish young offenders. *British Journal on Alcohol and Alcoholism, 17,* (4), 145/153.

Heather, N. (1986a). Minimal treatment interventions for problem drinkers. In G. Edwards, (Ed.), *Current issues in clinical psychology,* (Vol. 4). New York. Plenum Press.

Heather, N. (1986b). Change without therapists: The use of self-help manuals by problem drinkers. In W. R. Miller & N. Heather (Eds.), *Treating addictive behaviors: Processes of change.* New York. John Wiley & Sons.

Heather, N. & Robertson, I. (1981). *Controlled drinking.* London. Methuen.
Heather, N. & Robertson, I. (1983a). *Controlled drinking.* (rev. Ed.), London. Methuen.
Heather, N. & Robertson, I. (1983b). Why is abstinence necessary for the recovery of some problem drinkers? *British Journal of Addiction, 78,* 139/144.
Heather, N. & Robertson, I. (1985). *So you want to cut down your drinking?* Edinburgh. SHEG.
Heather, N. & Robertson, I. (1986). *Problem drinking: The new approach.* London. Penguin.
Heather, N. Whitton, B. & Robertson, I. (1986). Evaluation of a self-help manual for media-recruited problem drinkers: Six month follow-up results. *British Journal of Clinical Psychology, 25,* 19/34.
HEC (1985). *That's the limit.* London. Health Education Council.
Heller, N. B. Sterzel, W. W. Gill, A. D. Kilde, R. A. & Schimerman, S. R. (1975). Operation identification: An assessment of effectiveness. National Evaluation Program-Phase I summary report. Institute of Criminal Justice, Law Enforcement Assistance Administration. US Department of Justice, Washington DC. US Government Printing Office.
Heron, J. (1975). Six category intervention analysis. *Human Potential Research Project.* University of Surrey.
Hersen, M. (1978). Do behavior therapists use self-reports as major criteria? *Behavior Analysis and Modification, 2,* (4), 328/334.
Hershon, H. I. Cook, T. & Foldes, P. A. (1974). What shall we do with the drunkenness offender? *British Journal of Psychiatry, 124,* 327/335.
HMSO (1967). Criminal Justice Act. London.
HMSO (1968). Offences of Drunkenness. CMND, No. 3663. London.
HMSO (1969). The sentence of the court: A handbook for the courts on the treatment of offenders. London.
HMSO (1972). Criminal Justice Act. Part III 34. London.
HMSO (1986) Data Protection Act. Elizabeth II. Chapter 35. London.
Hodgson, R. J. & Rankin, H. J. (1976). Moderation of excessive drinking by one exposure. *Behavior Research and Therapy, 14,* 305/307.
Hodgson, R. J. & Rankin, H. J. (1982). Cue exposure and relapse prevention. In P. Nathan, & W. Hay, (Eds.), Case studies and behavior modification of alcoholism. New York. Plenum Press.
Hodgson, R. J., Rankin, H. J. & Stockwell, T.R. (1978) Craving and loss of control. In P. E. Nathan, G.A. Marlatt, & T. Loberg (Eds.), *Alcoholism: new directions in behavioral research and treatment.* New York. Plenum Press.
Hodgson, R. J., Stockwell, T. R. & Rankin, H. J. (1979). Can alcohol reduce tension? *Behavior, Research and Therapy, 17,* 459/466.
Hodgson, R. J., Stockwell, T. R., Rankin, H. J. & Edwards, G. (1978). Alcohol dependence: The concept, its utility and measurement. *British Journal of Addiction, 73,* 339/342.
Home Office (1982). Are you dying for a drink? *Alcohol Education Project.* Home Office. London.
Hood, R. & Sparks, R. (1970). *Key issues in criminology.* London. Weidenfield and Nicholson.
Hoogerman, D., Huntley, D., Griffiths, B., Petermann, H. & Koch, C. E. (1984). Effective early intervention for adolescents harmfully involved in alcohol and drugs. *Journal of the Florida Medical Association. April.* 227/232.
Howard, K. I., Krause, M. S. & Orlinsky, D. E. (1986). The attrition dilemma: Towards a new strategy for psychotherapy research. *Journal of Consulting and Clinical Psychology, 54,* (1), 106/110.

Hudson, J. (1977). Problems of measurement in criminal justice. In L. Rutman (Ed.), *Evaluation research methods: A basic guide*. Beverly Hills. California. Sage.

Iglehart, A. P. & Stein, M. P. (1985). The female offender: A forgotten client? *Social Casework: The Journal of Contemporary Social Work, March*, 152/159.

Ignatieff, M. (1978). *A just measure of pain: The penitentiary in the industrial revolution, 1750/1850*. London. MacMillan.

Igra, A. & Moos, R. N. (1977). Drinking among college students: A longitudinal study. *Social Ecology Laboratory Report*. Department of Psychiatry, Stanford University.

Jaffe, A. (1974). Spark: School rehabilitation through drug prevention programs. *Drug Forum, 3*, 137/147.

Jeffs, B. W. & Saunders, W. M. (1983). Minimising alcohol-related offences by enforcement of the existing licensing legislation. *British Journal of Addiction, 78*, 67/77.

Jellinek, E. M. (1960). *The disease concept of alcoholism*. New Haven, Connecticut.

Jesness, C. F. (1975). Comparative effectiveness of behavior modification and transactional analysis programs for delinquents. *Journal of Consulting and Clinical Psychology, 43*, 758/779.

Jessor, R. (1980). The perceived environment in psychological theory and research. In D. Magnusson (Ed.), *The situation: An interactional perspective*. Hillsdale, New Jersey. Erlbaum.

Jessor, R. (1987). Problem behaviour: Theory, psychosocial development and adolescent problem drinking. *British Journal of Addiction, 82*, 331/342.

Jessor, R. & Jessor, S. L. (1975). Adolescent development and the onset of drinking: A longitudinal study. *Journal of Studies on Alcohol, 36*, (1), 27/51.

Jessor, R. & Jessor, S. L. (1977) Problem behavior and psychosocial development: A longitudinal study in youth. New York. Academic Press.

Johnson, J. O., Gibson, L. & Linden, R. (1978). Alcohol and rape in Winnipeg. *Journal of Studies on Alcohol, 39*, 1887/1898.

Johnston, L., O'Malley, P. & Eveland, L. (1978). Drugs and delinquency: a search for causal connections. In Kandel, D. (Ed.), *Longitudinal research on drug use: Empirical findings and methodological issues*. Washington DC. Hemisphere. Wiley.

Kandel, D. (1975). The measurement of "ever-use" and "frequency-quantity" in drug use surveys. In J. Elnson & D. Nusco. (Eds.), *Operational definitions in socio-behavioral drug research*. New York. Holt, Rinehart and Winston.

Kandel, D. B. (1980). Drug and drinking behavior among youth. *Annual Review of Sociology, 6*, 235/285.

Kandel, D. B., Kessler, R. C. & Margulies, R. S. (1978). Adolescent initiation into stages of drug use: A developmental analysis. *Journal of Youth and Adolescence, 7*, 13/40.

Kandel, D. B., Trieman, D., Faust, R. & Single, E. (1976). Adolescent involvement in illicit drug use: A multiple classification analysis. *Social Forces, 55*, 438/458.

Kaplan, H. B. (1977). Antecedents of deviant responses: Predicting from a theory of deviant behavior. *Journal of Youth and Adolescence, 6*, 89/101.

Kaplan, H. B. (1978). Deviant behavior and self-enhancement in adolescence. *Journal of Youth and Adolescence, 7*, 253/277.

Karoly, P. & Kanfer, F. H. (1982). *Self management and behavior change: From theory to practice*. New York. Pergamon Press.

Kazdin, A. E. (1978). Evaluating the generality of findings in analogue therapy research. *Journal of Consulting and Clinical Psychology, 46*, 673/686.

Kazdin, A. E. (1986). Comparative outcome studies of psychotherapy: Methodological issues and strategies. *Journal of Consulting and Clinical Psychology, 54*, (1), 95/105.

Kazdin, A. E. & Wilcoxon, A. B. (1976). Systematic desensitization and non-specific treatment effects: A methodological evaluation. *Psychological Bulletin, 83,* 729/758.

Keller, M. (1980). Alcohol and youth. In M. Mayer & W. Filstead (Eds.), *Adolescence and alcohol.* Cambridge, Massachusetts. Ballinger.

Kelling, G. L. & Pate, T. (1981). A study of foot patrol: The Newark experiment. *Research Bulletin II,* 30/32. Home Office Research Unit. London.

Keyes, E. & Block, J. (1984). Prevalence and patterns of substance use among early adolescents. *Journal of Youth and Adolescence, 1,* 1/14.

Kilshaw, D. (1987). Personal communication.

Kim, S., Hoffman, I. R. & Pike, M. A. (1984). An outcome evaluation instrument for alcohol education prevention and intervention programs. *Journal of Drug Education, 14,* (4), 331/346.

Kinder, B. N., Pape, N. E. & Walfish, S. (1980). Drug and alcohol education programs: A review of outcome studies. *International Journal of Addictions, 15,* (7), 1035/1054.

Kraemer, H. C. (1981). Coping strategies in psychiatric clinical research. *Journal of Consulting and Clinical Psychology, 49,* 309/319.

Kuhn, T. S. (1962). *The structure of scientific revolutions.* Chicago. The University of Chicago Press.

Lanza-Kaduce, L., Akers, R. L., Krohn, M. D. & Rodosevich, M. (1984). Cessation of alcohol and drug use among adolescents: A social learning model. *Deviant Behavior, 5,* 79/96.

Larson, R. C. (1975). What happened to patrol operations in Kansas City? A review of the Kansas City Preventive Patrol Experiment. *Journal of Criminal Justice, 3,* 267/297.

Leathar, D. S. (1978). The self-monitoring of alcohol levels in Scotland. *Community Education, Winter, 1978/79,* 35/40.

Lenke, L. (1982). Alcohol and crimes of violence: A causal analysis. *Contemporary Drug Problems, Fall,* 355/365.

Leventhal, H. (1970). Findings and theory in the study of mass communications. In L. Berkowitz (Ed.), *Advances in experimental social psychology.* New York. Holt, Rinehart and Winston.

Lipton, E., Martinson, R. & Wilks, J. (1975). The effectiveness of correctional treatment: A survey of treatment evaluation studies. New York. Praeger.

Logan, C. H. (1972). Evaluation research in crime and delinquency: A reappraisal. *Journal of Criminal Law, Criminology and Police Science, 63,* (3), 378/387.

Luborsky, L. & Singer, B. (1975). Comparative studies of psychotherapies: Is it true that "Everyone has won and all must have prizes?" *Archives of General Psychiatry, 32,* 995/1008.

Lucker, G. W., Rosenfield, D., Sikes, J. & Aronson, E. (1976). Performance in the interdependent classroom: A field study. *American Education Research Journal, Spring 13,*(2) 115/123.

MacKay, J. R. (1963). Problem drinking among juvenile delinquents. *Crime and Delinquency, 9,* 19/38.

Mahoney, M. J. (1974). *Cognition and behavior modification.* Cambridge, Massachusetts. Ballinger.

Mahoney, M. J. (1979). Cognitive issues in the treatment of delinquency. In J. S. Stumphauzer (Ed.), Progress in behavior therapy with delinquents. Springfield. Illinois. C. C. Thomas.

Maisto, S. A., Sobell, M. B. & Sobell, L. C. (1979). Comparison of alcoholics' self-reports of drinking behavior with reports of collateral informants. *Journal of Consulting and Clinical Psychology, 47,* (1), 106/112.

Marlatt, G. A. & Miller, W. R. (1984). *Comprehensive drinker profile.* Odessa. Florida. Psychological Assessment Resources Inc.

Marlatt, G. A. & Parks, G. A. (1982). Self-management of addictive behaviors. In P. Karoly & F. H. Kanfer (Eds.), *Self-management and behavior change: From theory to practice.* New York. Pergamon Press.

Mayhew, P. M., Clarke, R. V., Sturman, A. & Hough, J. M. (1976). Crime as opportunity. *Home Office Research Study No. 34.* London. HMSO.

McCord, J. (1978). A thirty-year follow-up of treatment effects. *American Psychologist, March,* 284/289.

McFall, R. M. (1978). Smoking cessation research. *Journal of Consulting and Clinical Psychology, 46,* 703/712.

McGeorge, J. (1963). Alcohol and crime. *Medicine Science and Law, 3,* 27/48.

McGill, P., Williamson, P., Roberts, J. & Frith, R. (1987). An experimental alcohol programme for prisoners. *Probation Journal, March,* 61/67.

McGuire, E. (1969). The nature of attitudes and attitude change. In C. Lindzey & E. Aronson (Eds.), *The handbook of social psychology,* (Vol 3, 2nd Ed.). Cambridge, Massachusetts. Addison-Wesley.

McGuire, J. & Priestley, P. (1985). *Offending behaviour: Skills and stratagems for going straight.* London. Batsford Press.

McLaughlin, P. (1985). Police management of public drunkenness in Scotland. *British Journal of Criminology, 25,* (1), 344/364.

McLoone, P., Oulds, G. & Morris, J. (1987). Alcohol education groups: Compulsion v voluntarism. *Probation Journal, June,* 25.

McMullin, R. E. (1986). *Handbook of cognitive therapy techniques.* New York. W. W. Norton.

McMurran, M. (1988). Personal communication.

McMurran, M. & Baldwin, S. (1989) Services for prisoners with alcohol related problems: A survey of UK Prisons. *British Journal of Addictions. 84,* 1053/1058.

McMurran, M. & Boyle, M. (1990). Evaluation of a self-help manual for young offenders who drink: A pilot study. *British Journal of Clinical Psychology, 29,* 117/119.

Menary, R. (1986). Alcohol education programme for offenders. Taunton. Somerset Probation Service.

Menary, R. (1988). Personal communication.

Midanik, L. (1982). The validity of self-reported alcohol consumption and alcohol problems: A literature review. *British Journal of Addiction, 77,* 357/382.

Miller, W. R. (1976). Alcoholism scales and objective assessment methods: A review. *Psychological Bulletin, 83,* 649/674.

Miller, W. R. (1978). Behavioral treatment of problem drinkers: A comparative outcome study of three controlled drinking therapies. *Journal of Consulting and Clinical Psychology, 46,* 74/86.

Miller, W. R. (1983a). Motivational interviewing with problem drinkers. *Behavioural Psychotherapy, 11,* 147/172.

Miller, W. R. (1983b). Controlled drinking: A history and critical review. *Journal of Studies on Alcohol, 44,* 68/82.

Miller, W. R. (1985). Motivation for treatment: A review with special emphasis on alcoholism. *Psychological Bulletin, 98,* 84/107.

Miller, W. R. (1987a). Techniques to modify hazardous drinking patterns. In 425-438.

Miller, W. R. (1987b). Haunted by the Zeitgeist: Reflections on contrasting treatments goals and concepts of alcoholism in Europe and the United States. *Annals New York Academy of Sciences,* 110/128.

Miller, W. R. Crawford, V. L. & Taylor, C.A. (1979). Significant others as corroborative sources for problem drinkers. *Addictive Behaviors, 4,* 67/70.

Miller, W. R. & Hester, R. K. (1986). The effectiveness of alcoholism treatment: What research reveals. In W. R. Miller, & N. Heather, (Eds.), *Treating addictive behaviors: Process of change.* New York. Plenum Press.

Miller, W. R. & Munoz, R. F. (1976). How to control your drinking. Englewood Cliffs, New Jersey. Prentice-Hall.

Miller, W. R., Pechacek, T. F. & Hamburg, S. (1981). Group behavior therapy for problem drinkers. *The International Journal of Addiction, 16,* (5), 829/839.

Miller, W. R., Sovereign, R. G. & Krege, B. (1988). Motivational interviewing with problem drinkers: II The drinker's check up as a preventive intervention. *Behavioural Psychotherapy, 16,* 251/268.

Miller, W. R. & Taylor, C. A. (1980). Relative effectiveness of bibliotherapy, individual and group self-control training in the treatment of problem drinkers. *Addictive Behaviors, 15,* 13/24.

Miller, W. R., Taylor, C. A. & West, J. C. (1980). Focused versus broad-spectrum behavior therapy for problem drinkers. *Journal of Consulting and Clinical Psychology, 48,* 590/601.

Miller, B. A. & Welte, J. W. (1987). Comparisons of incarcerated offenders according to use of alcohol and/or drugs prior to offense. *Criminal Justice and Behavior 13(4),* 366/392.

Mitchell, J. N. (1971). *Alcohol and health: Special report to the US Congress.* D.H.E.W. Publications No. (HSM) 72-9099.

Moore, M. & Weiss, S. (1985). Alcohol and drunkenness-a newly developed curricular unit as a model for drug-education, science-oriented curricular programs. *Journal of Drug Education, 15,* (3), 263/271.

Morgan, H. G. & Hayward, A. (1976). The effects of drug talks to school children. *British Journal of Addiction, 71,* 285/288.

Moser, J. (1979). Prevention of alcohol-related problems: developing a broad-spectrum programme. *British Journal of Addiction, 74,* 133/140.

Myers, T. (1983). Corroboration of the self-reported alcohol consumption-a comparison of the accounts of a group of male prisoners and those of their wives/cohabitees. *Alcohol and Alcoholism, 18,* (1), 67/74.

Nathan, P. E. & Lansky, D. (1978). Common methodological problems in research on addictions. *Journal of Consulting and Clinical Psychology, 46,* 713/726.

Newman, R. (1971). Involuntary treatment of drug addiction. In P. Bourne (Ed.), *Addiction.* New York. Academic Press.

Nicholson, R. A. & Berman, J. S. (1983). Is follow up necessary in evaluation psychotherapy? *Psychological Bulletin, 93,* (2), 261/278.

Nilson-Giebel, M. (1980). Peer groups help prevent dependence. *International Journal of Health Education, 23,* 20/24.

NPS (1982). Corby Alcohol Therapy Group (1979/1981) Report. Northampton. Northamptonshire Probation Service.

Nylander, I. & Rydelius, P. A. (1973). The relapse of drunkenness in nonasocial teenage boys. *Acta Psychiatrica Scandinavia, 49,* 435/443.

O'Leary, K. D. & Borkovec, T. D. (1978). Conceptual, methodological and ethical problems of placebo group in psychotherapy research. *American Psychologist, 33,* 821/830.

Orford, J. (1973). A comparison of alcoholics whose drinking is totally uncontrolled and those whose drinking is mainly controlled. *Behavior Research and Therapy, 11,* 565/576.

Orford, J. (1986). *Excessive appetites: A psychological view of addiction.* London. Wiley.

Orford, J., Oppenheimer, E. & Edwards, G. (1976). Abstinence or control: The outcome for excessive drinkers two years after consultation. *Behavior Research and Therapy, 14,* 409/418.

Orne, M. T. (1962). On the social psychology of the psychological experiment. *American Psychologist, 17,* 776/783.

Out of Court (1982). Alternatives for drunkenness offenders: Dealing with drunkenness, a proposal for change. London. Out of Court.

Pallone, N. J. (1988). Substance abuse and felony crime. A question unsettled by discrepant methods of inquiry. (Manuscript submitted for publication).

Parlott, M. B. (1986). Placebo controls in psychotherapy research: A sine qua non or a placebo for research problems? *Journal of Consulting and Clinical Psychology, 54,* (1), 79/87.

Pattison, E. M. (1976). Nonabstinent drinking goals in the treatment of alcoholism. *Archives of General Psychiatry, 33,* 923/930.

Pattinson, E. M., Sobell, M. B. & Sobell, L. C. (1977). *Emerging concepts of alcohol dependence.* New York. Springer-Verlag Publishing.

Patton, M. Q. (1982). Creative evaluations. New York. Sage.

Patton, M. Q. (1983). Practical evaluations. New York. Sage.

Paul, G. (1976). Strategies of outcome research in psychotherapy. *Journal of Consulting Psychology, 31,* 109/118.

Pearce, J. & Garrett, H. D. (1970). A comparison of the drinking behavior of delinquent youth versus non-delinquent youth in the states of Idaho and Utah. *The Journal of School Health, 40,* 131/135.

Pernanen, K. (1982). Theoretical aspects of the relationship between alcohol use and crime. In J. J. Collins (Ed.), *Drinking and crime.* London. Tavistock Publications.

Pittman, D. J. (1968). Existing and proposed treatment facilities in the USA. Paper presented at International Symposium on "The Drunkenness Offence" Institute of Psychiatry. London.

Praill, T. & Baldwin, S. (1988). Beyond hero-innovation: Real change in unreal systems. *Behavioural Psychotherapy, 16,* 1/14.

Pratt, J. (1985). Delinquency as a scarce resource. *The Howard Journal of Criminal Justice, 24,* (2), 93/107.

Preusser, D. F., Ulmer, R. G., & Adams, J.. (1976). Driver record evaluation of a drinking driver rehabilitation program. *Journal of Safety Research, 8,* (3), 818/821.

Price, R. H. (1978). *Abnormal behavior: Perspectives in conflict.* New York. Holt, Rinehart and Winston.

Priestley, P. (1977). Victims: The key to penal reform. *Christian Action Journal, Summer,* 12/13.

Priestley, P., McGuire, J., Flegg, D., Hensley, V., Welham, D. & Barnitt, R. (1984). *Social skills in prisons and in the community.* London. Routledge and Kegan Paul.

Prins, H. A. (1973). *Criminal behaviour.* London. Pitman.

Prins, H. A. (1980). *Offenders, deviants or patients? An introduction to the study of socio-forensic problems.* London. Tavistock Publications.

Prochaska, J. O. & Di Clemente, C. C. (1982). Transthereotical therapy: Towards a more integrative model of change. *Psychotherapy: Theory, Research and Practice, 19,* 276/278.

Prochaska, J. O. & Di Clemente, C. C. (1986). Towards a comprehensive model of change. In N. Heather & W. R. Miller (Eds.), *Treating Addictive Behaviors: Process of Change.* New York. Plenum Press.

Rachman, S. & Hodgson, R. J. (1974). Synchrony and desynchrony in fear and avoidance. *Behavior Research and Therapy, 12,* 311/318.

Rada, R. T. (1975) Alcoholism and forcible rape. *American Journal of Psychiatry, 132,* 444/446.

Radzinowicz, L. & King, J. (1979). *The growth of crime: The international experience.* London. Hamish Hamilton.

Rankin, H., Hodgson, R. & Stockwell, T. (1983). One exposure and response prevention with alcoholics: A controlled trial. *Behavior, Research and Therapy, 21,* (4), 435/446.

Rapoport, L. (1961). The concept of prevention. *Social Work, 6,* 3/12.

Reilly, P. R., Cohen, R. B. & Lundy, N. A. (1974). Diagnostic interviewing with youthful offenders. *International Journal of Offender Therapy and Comparative Criminology, 18,* 153/158.

Remington, B. & Remington, M. (1987). Behavior modification in probation work: A review and modification. *Criminal Justice and Behavior, 14,* (2), 156/174.

Repucci, N. D. (1977). Implementation issues for the behavior modifier as institutional change agent. *Behavior Therapy, 8,* 594/605.

Repucci, N. D. & Saunders, C. D. (1974). The social psychology of behavior modification: Problems of implementation in natural settings. *American Psychologist, 29,* 649/660.

Rieken, H. W. & Boruch, R. F. (1974). *Social experimentation: A method for planning and evaluating social interventions.* New York. Academic Press.

Ritson, B. (1986). Merits of simple intervention. In W. R. Miller, & N. Heather, (Eds.). *Treating Addictive Behaviors: Process of Change.* New York. Plenum Press.

Rizvi, W. S., Hyland, E. & Blackstock, K. (1984). Some considerations for behavioral therapy in Scottish penal institutions. *International Journal of Offender Therapy and Comparative Criminology, 16,* 205/210.

Robertson, I. & Heather, N. (1982a). An alcohol education course for young offenders: A preliminary report. *British Journal on Alcohol and Alcoholism, 17,* 32/38.

Robertson, I. & Heather, N. (1982b). A survey of controlled drinking treatment in Britain. *British Journal on Alcohol and Alcoholism, 17,* (3), 102/105.

Robertson, I. & Heather, N. (1985). So you want to cut down your Drinking: A self-help guide to sensible drinking. Edinburgh. Scottish Health Education Group.

Robertson, I., Heather, N. Dzialowski, A., Crawford, J. & Winton, M. (1986). A comparison of minimal versus intensive controlled drinking treatment interventions for problem drinkers. *British Journal of Clinical Psychology, 25,* 185/194.

Robinson, D. (1972). The alcohologist's addiction: Some implications of having lost control over the disease concept of alcoholism, *Quarterly Journal of Studies on Alcohol, 33,* 1028/1042.

Robinson, C., Patton, J. & Kerr, W. (1965). A psychiatric assessment of criminal offenders. *Medicine, Science and Law, 5,* 140/146.

Roizen, J. & Schneberk, D. (1977). Alcohol and crime. In M. Aarens, T. Cameron, J. Roizen, R. Roizen, R. Room, D. Schneberk & S. Wingard (Eds.). *Alcohol Causalities and Crime.* Berkeley, California. Social Research Group.

Rogers, C. R. (1957). The necessary and sufficient conditions of therapeutic personality change. *Journal of Consulting Psychology, 21,* (2), 95/103.

Rogers, C. R. (1975) Empathic: An unappreciated way of being. *The Counselling Psychologist, 5,* (2), 2/10.

Room, R. (1980). Treatment-seeking populations and larger realities. In G. Edwards & M. Grant (Eds.). *Alcoholism treatment in transition.* London. Croom Helm.

Rosenthal, R. (1966). *Effects in behavioral research.* New York. Appleton-Century Crofts.

Rydelius, P. A. (1983a). Alcohol-abusing teenage boys: Testing a hypothesis on the relationship between alcohol abuse and social background factors, criminality and personality in teenage boys. *Acta Psychiatrica Scandinavia, 68,* 368/380.

Rydelius, P. A. (1983b). Alcohol-abusing teenage boys: Testing a hypothesis on alcohol abuse and personality factors, using a personality inventory. *Acta Psychiatrica Scandinavia, 68,* 381/385.

Sanchez-Craig, M. (1980). Random assignment to abstinence or controlled drinking in a cognitive-behavioral program: Short term effects on drinking behavior. *Addictive Behaviors, 5,* 35/59.

Sarason, I. G. (1978). A cognitive social learning approach to juvenile delinquency. In R. B. Hore & D. Schalling (Eds.). *Psychopathic behavior: Approaches to research.* New York. John Wiley & Sons.

Savage, S. (1988) Personal communication.

S. C. A. (1985a). *The enjoyable limit* (training video). Glasgow. Scottish Council on Alcohol.

S. C. A. (1985b). *Sensible drinking* (training video). Glasgow. Scottish Council on Alcohol.

Scheff, T. J. (1965). *Being mentally ill: A sociological theory.* Chicago. Aldine Press.

Schulz, R. & Harman-Hanusa, B. (1978). Long-term effects of control and predictability-enhancing interventions: Findings and ethical issues. *Journal of Personality and Social Psychology, 36,* (11), 1194/1201.

Schur, E. M. (1973). *Radical non-intervention: Rethinking the delinquency problem.* Englewood Cliffs, New Jersey. Prentice-Hall.

Schwartz, A. & Goldiamond, I. (1975). *Social casework: A behavioral approach.* New York. Columbia University Press.

Scioli, F. D. & Cook, T. J. (1975). *Methodologies for analysing public policy.* Lexington, Massachusetts. Lexington Books.

Scoles, P. & Fine, E. W. (1977). Short-term effects of an educational program for drinking drivers. *Journal of Studies on Alcohol, 38,* 633/637.

Scottish Council on Crime and Prevention of Crime (1975). Scottish Home and Health Department. Edinburgh. HMSO.

Shapiro, D. A. & Shapiro, D. (1983). Comparative therapy outcome research: Methodological implications of meta-analysis. *Journal of Consulting and Clinical Psychology, 51,* (1), 42/53.

Shaw, S. (1982). What is problem drinking? In M. A. Plant (Ed.). *Drinking and Problem Drinking.* London. Junction Books.

S.H.E.G. (1985a). *Drinkwise: A self-help guide and diary.* Edinburgh. Scottish Health Education Group.

S.H.E.G. (1985b). *Saturday night and Sunday morning* (training video). Edinburgh. Scottish Health Education Group.

S.H.E.G. (1985c). *Stand on your own two feet* (training video). Edinburgh. Scottish Health Education Group.

Sinclair, I. A. C., Shaw, M. & Troop, J. (1974). The relationship between introversion and response to casework in a prison setting. *British Journal of Social and Clinical Psychology, 13,* 51/60.

Singer, L. R. (1983). Trouble through drink: An evaluation of the Reading alcohol study group. Reading. Berkshire Probation Service.

Smart, R. (1976). *The new drinkers: Teenage use and abuse of alcohol.* (Vol 4). Toronto. Addiction Research Foundation of Ontario.

Smart, R. G. & Goodstadt, M. (1977). *Alcohol and drug use among Ontario students in 1977: Preliminary findings.* Toronto. Addiction Research Foundation.

Smith, R. (1982). The politics of alcohol. *British Medical Journal, 284,* 8 May, 1392/1395.

Sobell, M. B. & Sobell, L. C. (1973). Individualized behavior therapy for alcoholics. *Behavior Therapy, 4*, 49/72.

Sobell, L. C., Maisto, S. A. & Sobell, M. B. (1986). Comparison of alcoholics' self-reports of drinking behavior with reports of collateral informants. *Journal of Counselling and Clinical Psychology, 47*, (1), 106/112.

Sobell, M. B. & Sobell, L. C. (1976). Second year treatment outcome of alcoholics treated by individualized behavior therapy: Results. *Behavior Research and Therapy, 14*, 195/215.

Sobell, M. B. & Sobell, L. C. (1982). Controlled drinking: A concept of coming of age. In K. R. Blantain & J. Polivy (Eds.). *Self-control and self modification of emotional behavior.* New York. Plenum Press.

Sobell, L. C., Sobell, M. B. & Christelman, W. C. (1972). "The myth of 'one drink'." *Behavior Research and Therapy, 17*, 157/160.

Spence, S. (1979). Social skills training with adolescent offenders: A review. *Behavioural Psychotherapy, 7*, 49/56.

Spence, S. & Marzillier, J. S. (1979b). Social skills training with adolescent male offenders I. *Behavior, Research and Therapy, 17*, 7/16.

Spence, S. & Marzillier, J. S. (1981). Social skills training with adolescent male offenders II. Short-term, long-term and generalized effects. *Behavior, Research and Therapy, 19*, 349/368.

Stacey, B. & Davies, J. (1970). Drinking behavior in childhood and adolescence: An evaluative review. *British Journal of Addiction, 65*, 203/212.

Stacey, B. & Davies, J. (1972). The teenage drinker. *Education in the North, 9*, 1/7.

Stainback, R. D. & Rogers, R. W. (1983). Identifying effective components of alcohol abuse prevention programs: Effects of fear appeals, message style and source expertize. *International Journal of Addictions, 18*, (3), 393/405.

Staulcup, H., Kenward, K. & Frigo, D. (1979). A review of federal primary alcoholism prevention projects. *Journal of Studies on Alcohol, 40*, (11), 943/968.

Sterne, M. W., Pittman, D. J. & Coe, T. (1967). Teenagers, drinking and the law: A study of arrest trends for alcohol-related offenses. In D. Pittman (Ed.) *Alcoholism.* New York. Harper and Row.

Stevens, G. (1986) Personal communication.

Stiles, W. B., Shapiro, D. A. & Elliot, R. (1986). Are all psychotherapies equivalent? *American Psychologist, 41*, (2), 165/180.

Stockwell, T., Hodgson, R., Edwards, G., Taylor. C. & Rankin, H. (1979). The development of a questionnaire to measure the severity of alcohol dependence. *British Journal of Addiction, 74*, 79/87.

Stockwell, T., Murphy, D. & Hodgson, R. J. (1983). The severity of alcohol dependence questionnaire: Its use, reliability and validity. *British Journal of Addiction, 78*, 145/155.

Stokes, T. F. & Baer, D. M. (1977). An implicit technology of generalization. *Journal of Applied Behavior Analysis, 10*, 349/367.

Stuart, R. B. (1977). Behavioral contracting within the families of delinquents. *Journal of Behavior Therapy and Experimental Psychiatry, 2*, 1/11.

Stuart, R. B. (1974). Teaching facts about drugs: Pushing or preventing? *Journal of Educational Psychology, 66*, 189/201.

Stumphauzer, J. S. (1973). *Behavior therapy with delinquents.* Springfield, Illinois. C. C. Thomas.

Stumphauzer, J. S. (1979). *Progress in behavior therapy with delinquents.* Springfield, Illinois. C. C. Thomas.

Stumphauzer, J. S. (1980). Learning not to drink: Adolescents and alcohol. *Addictive Behaviors, 5,* 277/283.
Stumphauzer, J. S. (1981). Behavioral analyses of communities: A challenge. *Psychological Reports, 49,* 343/346.
Stumphauzer, J. S. (1982). Learning not to drink II: Peer survey of normal adolescents, *International Journal of Addictions, 17,* (8), 1363/1372.
Stumphauzer, J. S. (1983). Learning not to drink: Adolescents and abstinence. *Journal of Drug Education, 13,* (1), 39/48.
Stumphauzer, J. S. (1986). *Helping delinquents change.* New Brunswick, New Jersey. Transaction Books.
Stumphauzer, J. S., Veloz, E. V. & Aiken, T. W. (1981). Behavioral analyses of communities: A challenge. *Psychological Reports, 49,* 343/346.
Swenson, P. R. & Clay, T. R. (1980). Effects of short-term rehabilitation on alcohol consumption and drinking-related behaviors: An eight month follow-up study of drunken drivers. *The International Journal of Addictions, 13,* (5), 821/838.
Szasz, T. S. (1962). *The myth of mental illness.* London. Secker and Warberg.
Szasz, T. (1963). *Law, liberty and psychiatry.* New York. MacMillan.
Tate, D. (1985). New ventures: An offer of help to alcohol-related offenders. *Bulletin of the Scottish Legal Action Group, March,* 38/39.
Taylor, I., Walton, P. & Young, J. (1973). *Law and order: Arguments for socialism.* London. MacMillan.
Taylor, I., Walton, P. & Young, J. (1973). *The new criminology: For a social theory of deviance.* London. Routledge and Kegan Paul.
Tether, P. & Robinson, D. (1986). *Preventing alcohol problems: A guide to local action.* London. Tavistock Publications.
Tharp, R. G. & Wetzel, R. J. (1969). *Behavior modification in the natural environment.* New York. Academic Press.
Thoresen, C. E. & Mahoney, M. J. (1974). *Behavioral self-control.* New York. Holt Rinehart and Winston.
Thum, D., Wechsler, H. & Denone, H. (1973). Alcohol levels of emergency service patients injured in fights and assaults. *Criminology, 11,* 487/488.
Tittle, C. R. (1974). Prisons and rehabilitation: The inevitability of disfavour. *Social Problems, 21,* 385/395.
Trasler, G. (1974). The role of psychologists in the penal system. In H. Blom-Cooper (Ed.). *Progress in penal reform.* Oxford. Oxford University Press.
Trower, P., Bryant, M. & Argyle, M. (1978). *Social skills and mental health.* London Methuen. University Paperbacks.
Unterberger, H. & Di Ciccio, L. M. (1968). Alcohol education re-evaluated. *Bulletin of National Assessment in Secondary Schools Principals, 52,* 159/169.
US Bureau of Census (1978). Population characteristics. *Population Reports, 20.* 323. Table A. Washington DC. USGPO.
Vingilis, E. (1981). A literature review of the young drinking offender: Is he a problem drinker? *British Journal of Addiction, 76,* 27/46.
Virkkunen, M. (1974). Incest offences and alcoholism. *Medicine Science and the Law, 14,* (2), 124/128.
Vogler, R. E., Compton, J. V. & Weissbach, T. A. (1976). The referral problem in the field of alcohol abuse. *Journal of Community Psychology, 4,* 357/361.

Vogler, R. E., Weissbach, T. A., Compton, J. V. & Martin, G. T. (1977). Integrated behavior change techniques for problem drinkers in the community. *Journal of Consulting and Clinical Psychology, 45,* 267/279.

Ward, M. & Baldwin, S. (1990). Alcohol education courses in Forfar: A preliminary report. *Alcoholism Treatment Quarterly* Winter, 7,(4)

Warden, S. (1986) Personal communication.

Watson, C. G., Tilleskjor, C., Hoodecheck-Schow, E. A., Pucel, J. & Jacobs, L. (1983). Do alcoholics give valid self-reports? *Journal of Studies on Alcohol, 45,* (4), 344/348.

Wattenberg, W. W. & Moir, J. B. (1956). A study of teenagers arrested for drunkenness. *Quarterly Journal of Studies on Alcohol, 17,* 426/435.

Weiss, S. & Moore, M. (1986). Alcohol and drunkenness—a modular course. *Education in Chemistry, September,* 144/145.

West, D. J. (1980). The clinical approach to criminology. *Psychological Medicine, 10,* 619/631.

Wiener, R. S. P. (1970). *Drugs and school children.* London. Longman.

Williams, A. F., Di Ciccio, L. M. & Unterberger, J. H. (1968). Philosophy and evaluation of an alcohol education program. *Quarterly Journal of Studies on Alcohol, 29,* 685/702.

Winick, C. (1980). A theory of drug dependence based on role, access to, and attitudes towards drugs. In D. J. Lettieri et al., (Eds.). *Theories on drug abuse.* Rockville, Maryland. National Institute on Drug Abuse.

Winick, C. (1985). Specific targetting of prevention programs in alcohol and drug dependence. *The International Journal of Addiction, 20,* (4), 527/533.

Young, T. J. & Lawson, G. W. (1985). A. A. referrals for alcohol related-crimes: The advantages and limitations. *International Journal of Offender Therapy and Comparative Criminology,* 17, 131/139.

Zimring, F. E. (1976). Field experiments in general deterrance: Preferring the tortoise to the hare. *Evaluation, 3,* (1/2), 132/135.